How On Earth Can I Be Spiritual?

How On Earth Can I Be Spiritual?

by

C. SUMNER WEMP

THOMAS NELSON INC., PUBLISHERS
Nashville

All Scripture quotations are from the King James Version of the Bible.

Fifth Printing

Library of Congress Cataloging in Publication Data

Wemp, C Sumner.
  How on earth can I be spiritual?

  1. Spiritual life.   I. Title.
BV4501.2.W419   1978   248'.4   78-9035
ISBN 0-8407-9507-6

To those
whose enthusiastic response
and transformed lives,
my students,
made the writing of this book a
must and a joy

CONTENTS

PREFACE

How on earth can I be spiritual? This is the heart cry of millions of Christians. To will is present, but how to perform is as elusive as steam in the air.

Multitudes live a yo-yo Christian life, up one minute, down the next. The majority of believers are powerless. They have no real influence nor impact for God in their churches or communities. Most never win a soul to Christ. Few see miracles in answer to prayer. The Word of God is not real and exciting to read. There is no hunger for God. The fruit of the Spirit, love, joy, peace, is missing. There is a desperate need!

Thank God there is a great yearning for life-more-abundant sweeping the country. People are tired of staid, cold, callous "churchianity." Vast numbers are praying and pleading for a heaven-sent, heartfelt, Holy Ghost revival. We must have revival. God, to be sure, longs to send it.

In these chapters are the sane, sensible, scriptural truths of the Spirit-filled life and power for any individual, whether or not the churches and nations experience it. May God grant that these messages bring to your life that excitement and enthusiasm for God that is the normal, genuine Christian life.

Lynchburg, Virginia   C.S.W.
Spring, 1978

FOREWORD

In the spring of 1978 I preached at one of the largest Baptist churches in the state of Texas, Allandale Baptist in Austin. The pastor, Rev. Harold O'Chester, testified that Sumner Wemp's preaching on the Holy Spirit had changed his life. He went on in glowing terms to explain how many pastors are now coming to emphasize the deeper spiritual life, but how he had been preaching on the power of the Holy Spirit for years. He testified that powerful preaching on the Christian life by Sumner Wemp had given him the ability to build such a great church.

The night I returned from Texas, Sumner phoned and asked if I would write the foreword to this book. I told him I wanted to see the manuscript. I felt I had to read the book after hearing such a radiant commendation only a day earlier.

After reading *How on Earth Can I Be Spiritual* I felt every Christian ought to read it. Why? Because its message is both practical and scriptural. The illustrations and the honest approach to difficult questions make the book practical. But it also has Scripture. I believe Sumner deals with every major verse in the Bible that mentions the Holy Spirit.

Perhaps the best reason why you should read the book is the life behind the pages. This topic is not theoretical to Sumner Wemp. He is a radiant Christian who always smiles.

I once asked him if he ever frowns. "Not outwardly," he answered.

His answer contains the key to the spiritual life taught in this book. It shows we can be happy if we work at it, but there will be moments of disappointment.

But we should not let our defeats get us down, nor should we let them contaminate others. When we fail, because we are human, Sumner Wemp teaches us to find God's remedy, then go our way rejoicing.

If you know Sumner, he is always encouraging others with the phrase "bless the Lord." That's a good prayer for this book. As you read *How On Earth Can I Be Spiritual,* you will grow and ". . . bless the Lord."

Sincerely yours in Christ,

Elmer Towns
Lynchburg, Virginia
Spring, 1978

1
What on Earth Is a Spiritual Christian?

What in the world do you really want out of life? Forget religious things for a moment. Can you guess what a group of 600 college students said they wanted more than anything else out of life? Can you imagine that a group of 350 adults wanted the same things? Would you believe that 100 high schoolers gave the same top priorities as the others? Having asked scores of groups the same question, I have been astounded that three out of the first four answers were always the same! What would you name as the most important things you really want out of life?

The one most frequently named first is "happiness" or "joy." Everyone wants life to be filled with joy. College students usually answer they want "love"—deep, warm, abiding love. Many adults also name this first. Adults, especially the elderly, name "security" or "peace" first. Most of the time these are the first three answers given to the question, "What do you really want out of life?"

WHAT GOD WANTS

God says, "The fruit of the Spirit is love, joy, peace . . ." (Gal. 5:22). Isn't that amazing? The very things that people admire the most, God says He wants to produce first. Most people don't believe that! They believe to yield to God means giving up fun, living a drab life, being looked down on, and feeling sorry for yourself. Not so! Jesus said, "I want you to have life and have it abundantly" (John 10:10). Most people live such subnormal lives that when someone lives a normal Christian life, people think he is abnormal! The normal Christian life (not the usual, though) is a life filled with love and joy and peace. The world at its worst needs Christians at their best.

Make no mistake, these are not personality traits. These are not natural qualities. They are produced by the Holy Spirit. Satan has brainwashed Christians to excuse their lack of these qualities by saying they are "personality traits." No. The Holy Spirit produces them, and they are available to every Christian. One who lacks these is not only blind and cannot see afar off (see 2 Pet. 1:9), but he is denying the power of God in his life. It is a sin not to possess these characteristics in one's life.

Now, if these qualities produced by the Holy Spirit are described as the natural qualities of life that one has because he is a "choleric" personality type, then others are off the hook and can make up their excuses for unkindness or unhappiness. If, however, genuine love is produced by the Holy Spirit and every Christian possesses the Holy Spirit, then there is no excuse for a lack of love or joy or peace, is there? Christians need to be brought face to face with this fact and need to learn how to let the Holy Spirit take over and turn out tons of love and joy in their lives. Bless God, it is possible for every Christian to be full of joy (see 1 John 1:4) and rejoice always (see Phil. 4:4). Let's look at the whole list of fruit the Holy Spirit produces.

1. Love

"The love of God is shed abroad in our hearts by the Holy Ghost which is given unto us," declared Paul in Romans 5:5. This is not some cheap, sensual, selfish love that doesn't last. This is a deep, warm, soul-satisfying love that every heart craves. The most natural desire in the world is to love and be loved. The magic of existence is to be loved by even one person.

A little boy was asked why he passed up many churches and missions to come to Mr. Moody's Sunday school. "Because they love a fellow over there," was his reply.

God's love is lasting and unselfish. "Having loved his own which were in the world, he loved them unto the end" (John 13:1). Peter found this out for sure, for God forgave him and used him mightily, even though he had stumbled. My, how it improves people when we begin to love them.

Even the mob who put Jesus on the cross heard Him cry out, "Father, forgive them; for they know not what they do" (Luke 23:34). This same love is available in abundance to every believer.

2. Joy

"These things have I written unto you that your joy might be full" is the promise of God (see 1 John 1:4). Isn't that an exciting promise? He doesn't offer just a little teaspoonful of joy down in the bottom of the cup, but "fulness" of joy. This promise is for both here and hereafter, for the psalmist declares, "In thy presence is fulness of joy; at thy right hand there are pleasures for evermore" (Ps. 16:11). What more can you want?

Most people run around having a little fun doing this or a little fun doing that. Even the words themselves, "joy" and "fun," have an enormous difference in connotation in their very sound, don't they? It is one thing to enjoy the pleasures of sin for a season (see Heb. 11:25), but the headaches and hangovers just aren't worth it. Are you having a good time? You ought to. God made us to "rejoice always" (Phil. 4:4). Remember, this joy is a product of the Holy Spirit.

3. Peace

"Peace I leave with you, my peace I give unto you: not as the world giveth, give I unto you. Let not your heart be troubled neither let it be afraid," promised the Lord Jesus (John 14:27). This world could stand a good dose of peace, couldn't it? Many people have peace as long as their bank account holds up and their health doesn't break down. Let these slip away from them, and they crack up. Men ignore the peace of God for the pleasures of this world. God gives peace "which passeth all understanding" (Phil. 4:7) and "misunderstanding" as well. With the boom in tranquilizers (two billion pills per year), someone ought to tell the world about this free offer! A well-stocked supply of this could save a lot of fifty-dollar-an-hour visits to the psychiatrist as well. Don't look so troubled. You don't have to. A man said, "Nobody knows the trouble I've seen, but I keep trying to tell them." There are too many in the same boat today, and they are all about to sink.

4. Longsuffering

That's not the half of it, for the next fruit is "longsuffering" or "patience." Has your patience been wearing thin? Finding it hard to "keep your cool" these days? Have you had one of those Excedrin headaches lately? This fruit is the same "longsuffering to us-ward" that God has, "not willing that any should perish" (2 Pet. 3:9), and that leads us to repentance (see Rom. 2:4). If His longsuffering can take all the mistreatment of this world, and He can still "so love the world, that he gave his only begotten Son, that whosoever believeth in him should not perish, but have everlasting life" (John 3:16), maybe we each ought to get our own supply.

5. Gentleness

"Gentleness" or "kindness" is the next fruit hanging on the tree. We still celebrate "Be Kind to Dumb Animals Week," but all people need a little of the "milk of human kindness" toward one another. The Golden Rule is of no use unless you realize it is your move. Here is the one quality that is most rewarding and heartwarming. When it comes to doing for others, some people stop at nothing. Each of us has experienced the satisfying joy of showing kindness toward others, especially at Christmastime. It isn't hard to have this pleasure for a regular diet when the Holy Spirit is allowed to grow this fruit in our lives.

6. Goodness

"Goodness" or "generosity" is another fruit that grows in abundance on the "branches" of spiritual Christians. Some know the thrill of 2 Corinthians 9:7, which says, "Every man according as he purposeth in his heart, so let him give; not grudgingly, or of necessity: for God loveth a cheerful giver." Only the grace of God can effect this generosity. God says we are to work "that we may have to give to him that needeth" (Eph. 4:28). We make a living by what we get; we make a life by what we give. This is a fruit and grace of life produced only by the free flowing of the Spirit of God through the life of a Christian.

A great number of Christian works suffer because so few know the choice fruit of generosity. In the Old Testament, when Moses gathered material for the tabernacle, the Israelites, just out of bondage from Egypt, gave so much that Moses had to stop them, for he had more than enough. Wouldn't it be fantastic for a pastor to have that problem today!

7. Faithfulness

"Faith," or "faithfulness," as the Greek really states, grows on the trees "planted by the rivers of water, that bringeth forth his fruit in his season" (Ps. 1:3). God says, "Be thou faithful unto death" (Rev. 2:10), and again, "It is required in stewards, that a man be found faithful" (1 Cor. 4:2). There are so many with so much who do so little for lack of this fruit. How refreshing to see a couple who have been faithful and devoted to each other enough to celebrate a silver or golden anniversary. Their children indeed shall call them blessed and not curse them. The faithfulness for this comes from allowing the Holy Spirit to produce the fruit of faithfulness. Many people go in spurts and squirts. They have a malaria type of Christianity, a fever and a chill, hot one minute and cold the next. We are in a marathon, not a hundred-yard dash, and the race requires steady going. Let the Spirit of God make you faithful and establish you.

8. Meekness

"The meek . . . shall inherit the earth" (Matt. 5:5). Meekness or gentleness or humility, as the Greek expresses it, is a much-needed quality of life. "Humility and How I Obtained It in Seven Easy Lessons" has been suggested as a title of a book! Who would read it? "When thou wast little in thine own sight . . ." (1 Sam. 15:17) is a good description of meekness. Few people are big enough to become small enough for God to use. It is surprising how those with this fruit can rise to the top. This fruit does so much to preserve unity and harmony in a home or office, for a "soft answer turneth away wrath" (Prov. 15:1). Need a little? Get with the "in" crowd. The more we are humbled by grace, the more we shall be exalted in glory.

9. Temperance

"Temperance" is advocated even by distilleries. They certainly don't get good publicity for their product by those "controlled by" or "under the influence of" alcohol. Temperance means "self-control" or, better still, "control of self." This doesn't mean willpower; it means to be "controlled by" or "filled with" the Holy Spirit.

The comparison is made in Ephesians 5:18, "And be not drunk with wine, wherein is excess; but be filled with the Spirit." See the comparison? Don't be under the influence of alcohol; be under the influence of the Holy Spirit. He can control us to the extent that "every thought is brought into captivity to the obedience of Christ" (2 Cor. 10:5).

Fantastic promise, isn't it? Many can testify to the reality of this in their lives. Our faults are more pardonable than the excuses we use to hide them. Have cheer, there's hope. You, too, can have this fruit in your life.

Suppose I run over to a piano and frantically bang away on the keys. You ask, "What's the matter?" and I reply, "I'm thirsty—I'm about to choke; I want a drink of water." Then I rush over to a string of light switches and flip them on and off. Again you ask, "What's the matter?" Again I reply, "I'm thirsty and want a drink." Off again I go to a TV set and furiously turn knobs and dials. Once again you ask, and once again I answer, "I'm thirsty." About now you would cry out, "Go to the water fountain! That's where you get water. You will never get it from these other things." So it is with this wonderful and much-desired fruit of love, joy, peace. Quit running to the myriad of things in the world; they will never produce this fruit. Go to the Holy Spirit; He alone produces this fruit.

EVIDENCES OF POWER

God promises, "Ye shall receive power, after that the Holy Ghost is come upon you: and ye shall be witnesses unto me" (Acts 1:8).

Witnessing

Another proof of a Spirit-filled Christian or of spirituality is power to witness and power in witnessing. It is significant that God did not say, "After that the Holy Spirit is come upon you, and ye shall pray or ye shall study the Bible intensely." These are, of course, important, but a result of the Holy Spirit upon a person is that he becomes a witness. Can we use this criterion today? It certainly was true all through the Book of Acts. A good outline of Acts is: Chapter 1, the Savior went up; chapter 2, the Spirit came down; and chapters 3ff., the saints went out. This is God's pattern. Just as true as the number two follows the number one, so witnessing follows Spirit-filled living. Dr. Charles Ryrie pointed out in his book *Balancing the Christian Life* that every place in the Book of Acts where people were filled with the Spirit, they were witnessing!

The Man of Galilee said, "Follow me, and I will make you fishers of men" (Matt. 4:19). If you are not fishing for men, you are not following the Savior. Doesn't it follow if you are not witnessing for the Savior, you are not filled with the Spirit? We each should search our souls on this matter.

Greater Works

"He that believeth on me, the works that I do shall he do also; and greater works than these shall he do" (John 14:12) is the staggering but stimulating promise of Jesus. Now, don't quibble about what He means by "greater works." Is there anything in your life that evidences the supernatural power of God working through you? Spirituality is not a stagnant, dormant life, with you acting holier than someone else. We too "must work the works of him that sent us" (John

19

9:4) and must go "into all the world, and preach the gospel" (Mark 16:15).

Lack of Fear

"God hath not given us the spirit of fear; but of power, and of love, and of a sound mind" (2 Tim. 1:7). Over and over people confess they do not witness because of "fear." To be sure, this fear doesn't come from God, for "God hath not given us the spirit of fear," and that's that. Fear is a product of self and Satan. It comes out of dependence on self or the deception of Satan. The one sure cure is to let the Holy Spirit do what He came to do: control us.

"And with great power gave the apostles witness of the resurrection of the Lord Jesus: and great grace was upon them all" (Acts 4:33). Have you ever noticed that a drunken man has no fear even of someone much larger than he? He will take on anyone. When one is not drunk with wine, but filled with the Holy Spirit, he loses his fear and has power to witness. Paul feared men so little because he feared God so much. "The arm of flesh will fail you." Your knees will smote one another. But God has promised power to witness. Perhaps "you have not because you ask not."

Love

"No man cared for my soul" (Ps. 142:4) is without doubt one of the saddest statements a man ever made. People around you will go to bed with a broken heart tonight and feel this empty loneliness. Many will die and go to hell without one Christian loving them for one minute. Can you spare a little love? Have you gotten your share of love from the Spirit? It's a promise!

Sound Mind

"Therefore [reasoned] he in the synagogue with the Jews" (Acts 17:17). Yes, you too have a sound mind, a reasoning mind, from the Holy Spirit. You too are without excuse. God is reasonable (Isa. 1:18). The gospel is so simple a child can understand it and is bidden to come (Matt. 18:3; 19:14).

"Why stand ye gazing up into heaven?" (Acts 1:11). Let's get with it.

Power in Witnessing

"And when he [the Holy Spirit] is come, he will reprove [convict] the world of sin" (John 16:8). No wonder when they witnessed, the people "were pricked in their heart" (Acts 2:37), "they were cut to the heart" (Acts 5:33; 7:54), "and the Lord added to the church daily such as should be saved" (Acts 2:47). God is not dead. The Lord Jesus promised results: "I have . . . ordained you, that ye should . . . bring forth fruit, and that your fruit should remain" (John 15:16). Fruit here surely includes souls, for the context of Romans 1:13–16 certainly indicates that fruit here came from preaching the gospel, and souls were saved.

Every Christian should be a soul-winner. Witnessing is not a gift; it is a command! Soul-winning is not like something in a cafeteria that you can take or leave. It is every Christian's job. God has promised power. He has also promised results, so "let us not be weary in well doing: for in due season we shall reap, if we faint not" (Gal. 6:9). The Holy Spirit has to convince, convict, and convert, but God's plan has always been to use man. God could have saved the Ethiopian eunuch, but the Spirit sent Philip. The eunuch, when asked if he understood what he read, said: "How can I, except some man should guide me?" (Acts 8:31). Will you be that man? One walking in the Spirit will be sent to souls, as was Philip. "O foolish Galatians, who hath bewitched you, that ye should not obey the truth?" (Gal. 3:1). This could surely be asked of multitudes of Christians today who just sit, soak, and sour.

Boldness

"Now when they saw the boldness of Peter and John, and perceived that they were unlearned and ignorant [had not been to seminary] men, they marvelled" (Acts 4:13). Where did Peter, stumbling and fumbling, get such boldness? "When they had prayed [for boldness], the place was shaken where they were assembled together; and they were all filled with the Holy Ghost, and they spake the word of God with boldness" (Acts 4:31). Could you use a little more boldness? Why not try this little formula: Ask for it (Acts 4:29) and let the Holy Spirit do what He came to do through you! Try the "pray as you go" plan.

PRAISE THE LORD

"Let every thing that hath breath praise the Lord" (Ps. 150:6). It was so real, seemed so natural, as a Christian spoke out during the special music, "Praise Jesus." You may not shout "amen" in a service, but you should have a genuine shout in your heart if you are a Spirit-filled Christian. There should be a deep longing to glorify the Lord Jesus. Remember the Halo shampoo slogan, "It glorifies your hair." A spirit-controlled Christian will *glorify* the Lord Jesus. He will have the preeminence (see Col. 1:18). Who is prominent in your church? In your life? In some places it's Mary, or Mary Baker Eddy, or some "gift" of the Spirit, or some denomination. If the Holy Spirit is behind it, you can be sure the Lord Jesus Christ will be prominent.

A pastor preached on what the Bible had to say about marriage and divorce. He preached how God had a plan for one man and one woman to be married until death parted them. In the course of the message he pointed out that to be married and divorced and remarried just was not God's plan. After the service a lady who had never married said she wanted to talk to him about the message. Fearing that she might have disapproved of his message, he quickly said, "Now, God has a plan, and you cannot change God's plan nor improve on it." She stopped him and said, "Pastor, I don't want to change God's plan; I just want to get in on it!"

God has a plan for living. It is to have life and have it more abundantly. Why don't you get in on it?

Study Questions: Chapter 1

1. What do most people say they really want out of life, and where does what they want come from?
2. What is the difference between human personality and the fruit of the Spirit?
3. Discuss the fruit of the Spirit.
4. What does the power of the Holy Spirit accomplish in the believer's life?

2
What on Earth Does the Spirit Do?

The Holy Spirit came at Pentecost to take up where the Savior left off, but today most Christians don't realize that. The Lord Jesus suffered, died, rose again, went back to heaven, sat down, and sent the Spirit to take over the work of God on earth. This is the day of the Holy Spirit. (See Figure 1.)

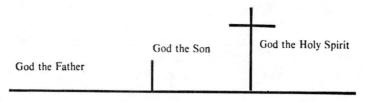

Figure 1.

All through the Old Testament the prominent person working on earth was God the Father, the almighty One. When the Lord Jesus Christ came, He was the prominent One at work here on earth. Today the Holy Spirit is the prominent One at work in carrying out the plan and purpose of God on earth. We need to recognize this. Many people falter in their Christian lives because they are not consciously depending on the Holy Spirit to do to and through them what He came to do.

THE SPIRIT'S TAKEOVER

What a startling announcement it was in John 14 when Jesus told His disciples He was going away. Questions came fast and furiously. What were they to do? Fear seemed to grip their hearts. Then the Lord Jesus made a most encouraging statement: "I will pray the Father, and he shall give you another Comforter, that he may abide with you forever; even the Spirit of truth; whom the world cannot receive, because it seeth him not, neither knoweth him: but ye know him; for he dwelleth with you, and shall be in you" (John 14:16,17).

The Lord Jesus had been ministering, teaching, leading, and walking with His disciples for three years. Now He was about to finish the work He came to do, to be crucified, to bear the sins of the world in His own body on the cross, be buried, and rise again. Then He was to go back to the Father. This gospel then was to be carried into all the world (Matt. 28:19,20). While here in His body, the Lord Jesus could be in only one place at a time and was therefore limited to ministering to those in that one place.

The disciples had been with Him constantly, and the question now was who would teach them and lead them after He left? He told them, "I'll send another Comforter." The Greek word for "another" means "another of the same kind," as He Himself was, with infinite wisdom and power. Who was this other Comforter? Why, the Holy Spirit, the Spirit of Truth. He was not coming to live in only one body as the Lord Jesus did, but was especially prepared to live in each believer. The Holy Spirit all through the past had been *with* the disciples and the people of God, but now He "shall be *in* you," declared the Lord. What a revolutionary truth! Not only that, but in contrast to the Lord Jesus leaving them, the Holy Spirit was to abide forever! (See Figure 2.)

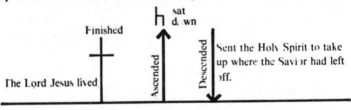

Figure 2.

Fit all this together with Hebrews 1:3. Speaking of the Lord Jesus, God said, "When he had by himself purged our sins, sat down on the right hand of the Majesty on high." One searching question needs an answer: Why did the Lord Jesus sit down? The simple answer is, He was finished. He had come to be the Savior. He had finished all His work in being the Savior, and He went back to the Father and sat down. Then forty days later the Holy Spirit came to take up where the Savior had left off.

This is the most transforming truth a believer can ever get hold of. Tragically, judging from hymns, sermons, books, and talk most Christians are not consciously aware of the fullness of this truth. Most are still looking to, asking for, and depending on the Lord Jesus to do the very things He sent the Holy Spirit to do. If Christians would begin to look to, ask for, and depend on the Holy Spirit to do the things the Scriptures tell us are His responsibility and ministry today, their lives would be transformed.

From a parallel, let's try to get in our minds the picture of God's work as He planned it. If a college student went into the business office and asked to see his grades, the accountant would say, "You are seeing the wrong person; go to the academic office—that's their job." If one went into the academic dean's office to ask about his bill, the dean would say he was in the wrong office and direct him to the business office. Now, there is no jealousy among these different officials in a school. Neither is inferior to the other. It is simply that each has a different responsibility. So it is with the Trinity. There is no jealousy or inferiority between the Lord Jesus and the Holy Spirit, but each has a different ministry and responsibility.

Christians do not witness to non-Christians about the Holy Spirit to try to get them saved. They tell about the Lord Jesus and His work. He is the Savior. A lost person needs to know who the Savior is and what He came to do and then let the Savior save him. And Christians need to be told who the Holy Spirit is and what He came to do. Then they need to let the Holy Spirit do what He came to do in their lives. This is both profound and simple. It is the key to the joyous, victorious life.

POSSESSING THE SPIRIT

Just what did the Holy Spirit come to do? Begin in Romans 8:9: "Now if any man have not the Spirit of Christ, he is none of his." A person who has let the Savior do what He came to do—save him—has the Holy Spirit, for the Holy Spirit enters into his body the moment he is saved. If someone doesn't have the Holy Spirit, "he is none of his." He isn't saved. A Christian may not be aware that the Holy Spirit lives in his body, even as Paul had to instruct the new and untaught Christians at Corinth: "What? know ye not that your body is the temple of the Holy Ghost which is in you . . ." (1 Cor. 6:19). These were "carnal" Christians (1 Cor. 3:3), not some super-sanctified or spiritual Christians, but they too had the Holy Spirit.

Christians must be biblically correct. It is unscriptural to exhort a believer to "receive the Holy Spirit," for he already has the Holy Spirit. The proper exhortation is for the believer to let the Holy Spirit have him or let the Holy Spirit control him.

Again, it is totally unscriptural to exhort a believer, a born-again Christian, to "be baptized by the Holy Spirit," "for by one Spirit are we all [believers] baptized into one body" (1 Cor. 12:13). Again, these were carnal Christians, yet they had already been baptized by the Holy Spirit.

This is how one is "in Christ." He is "baptized" or "immersed" into one body, into Christ, and thus he is a new creature: For "if any man be in Christ, he is a new creature: old things are passed away; behold, all things are become new" (2 Cor. 5:17).

Make no mistake about it. Every Christian possesses the Holy Spirit. The Christian needs to let the Holy Spirit possess him. This is the scriptural teaching that must be made clear.

When the ministry of the Holy Spirit is properly understood and taught, "He shall glorify me" (John 16:14), said the Lord Jesus. The Lord Jesus is to have preeminence in everything (Col. 1:18). For Him to be glorified and have preeminence in one's life, the Holy Spirit must do it—and He will, once He is given His proper place in a believer's life. It is not a worked-up or self-induced effort; the ministry of the Holy Spirit is to glorify Christ through believers. *The proper teaching and emphasis on the Holy Spirit always results in glory to Christ.*

One other point needs to be clarified. God declares, "Christ in you, the hope of glory" (Col. 1:27). Also, "Christ liveth in me" (Gal. 2:20), said Paul. But, frankly, how does He do it? The Savior is in a body at the right hand of the Father.

The answer is simple and given to us in Ephesians 2:19–22. God tells us that all believers, "fitly framed together groweth unto an holy temple in the Lord, in whom ye also are builded together for an habitation of God *through the Spirit*" (italics mine). Christ does it in the Person of the Holy Spirit. So once again the Trinity, that great mystery of "he that hath seen me hath seen the Father" (John 14:9), comes to light.

All of the Trinity are operative today even as in other ages, but the Holy Spirit is the One operating prominently. In the Old Testament it was the God of Abraham, Isaac, and Jacob who was prominent. Then while Christ was on earth, He was prominent in the ministry of God. Now it is the Holy Spirit who is prominent in the ministry of God on earth. He, of course, turns our attention immediately to Christ when He is allowed to minister properly.

CONQUERING THE FLESH

In Romans 8:13 God says, "If ye through the Spirit do mortify the deeds of the [flesh]. . . ." How does one conquer the flesh and its passions? Not by crucifying himself in a deep struggle of self-denial, but in a conscious yielding to the control of the Holy Spirit. The "fruit of the Spirit is . . . temperance [self-control]" (Gal. 5:22,23).

Oh, how many go down in defeat trying "to put to death the deeds of the flesh" without a conscious looking to and dependence on the One the Savior sent to do it for them—the

Holy Spirit. Just as many people try through all kinds of deeds to save themselves, many Christians try through all kinds of deeds to control or crucify the flesh, instead of letting the Holy Spirit, who came to do it, accomplish it for them.

Some who "quit this" and "give up that" and "don't go here or there" become self-righteous and pharisaical about it. When one depends on the Holy Spirit and realizes He has accomplished the degree of sanctification that is in a person's life, he cannot "glory in the flesh," but will glorify the Lord Jesus. This can easily be the answer to those with a holier-than-thou attitude. Too much work is done by Christians in the energy of the flesh, and you can detect that it does not radiate Christ but exalts that person instead.

I smoked for eight months after I was saved. During that time I tried to quit scores of times. Once I tore up a whole pack of cigarettes one at a time, saying over and over again, "I hate you, I hate you." Surely, I thought, through this psychology I would stop, but an hour later I bought another pack. I struggled to quit and failed. At 4:00 A.M. on January 1, 1941, after being up all night at a New Year's Eve party, I cried out to God with a broken, desperate heart, "O God, You take them out of me." Bless the Lord, I never touched another cigarette. No way can I say that I quit. No way could the flesh get any glory from it. God did it all. That's the way He wanted it all along, that "no flesh should glory in his presence" (1 Cor. 1:29).

LED BY THE SPIRIT

"For as many as are led by the Spirit of God . . ." (Rom. 8:14). I love great gospel songs. John W. Peterson, a personal friend of mine, has written a song that is one of my favorites, "Jesus Led Me All the Way." There is a sense in which the Savior leads us through example. Indirectly He leads us, but it is directly by the Spirit. Christians, then, need to be scripturally correct by looking to and depending on the Holy Spirit to lead them.

What an exhilarating and humbling experience it is to see

the Holy Spirit truly leading in one's life. One night my wife and I went visiting for our church. She had been given four names and addresses of people we planned to visit. Before we left, we prayed that the Holy Spirit would lead us to someone prepared to be saved.

As we were on our way, we came to a stop sign. In the next block to our left was a service station operated by Gene, a Christian we knew. The Holy Spirit impressed my heart to run by for just a minute to encourage him, for he had been having some problems. While we were there, a man's name came up in conversation. I had witnessed to this man, who also operated a service station, and had been quite burdened to see him saved.

Gene excitedly said, "Why, he lives right down the street."

I again felt a deep urge and burden to go by and see him. When we knocked at the door, his wife answered. We introduced ourselves and were invited in quickly because it was five degrees below zero. He was at work, she said. After a few minutes of light talk, I began witnessing to her. As I spoke of Christ suffering for her sins, she burst into tears.

I said, "God has been dealing with you, hasn't He?" She nodded yes. When I finished she joyfully bowed her head and received the Lord Jesus and was gloriously saved. About an hour later, as we began to leave, she startled me by saying, "I knew you were coming tonight."

I said, "How could you? I didn't know you existed; you didn't know I existed. We didn't plan to come here." Then I told her how we had happened to come.

She replied, "I know all that; I've prayed all day God would send someone tonight to tell me how to be saved." Glory! This is the thrill and reality of the Holy Spirit leading one's life.

THE SPIRIT OF ADOPTION

"For ye have not received the spirit of bondage again to fear; but ye have received the Spirit of adoption, whereby we cry, Abba, Father" (Rom. 8:15). How does a Christian enter into that personal and close fellowship with God, to call Him "Abba, Father"? Paul said it is the "Spirit of adoption, whereby we cry, Abba, Father."

There doesn't seem to be an overwhelming number of people who have an intimate fellowship with the Father. Their prayers often seem so distant. God seems so far away and so unreal. Others talk to and about the Father in such a personal way that you feel they have already seen Him face to face. This deeply personal relationship comes through the Holy Spirit when He is allowed to produce it.

ASSURANCE OF SALVATION

Then, "the Spirit himself beareth witness with our spirit, that we are the children of God" (Rom. 8:16). Many Christians struggle for years with a lack of assurance of salvation. How does one get that deep-settled assurance in the very recesses of his soul? Once again the Holy Spirit is the One with this ministry. There is no jealousy, no conflict of interest, but it just makes sense that if some would look to the Holy Spirit, whose ministry this is, instead of vaguely praying or asking the Lord Jesus to do it, they might find that same witness borne in their hearts.

HELP IN PRAYER

"Likewise the Spirit also helpeth our infirmities: . . . [making] intercession for us with groanings which cannot be uttered" (Rom. 8:26). It is a common admission that most persons have a weak prayer life. Too often Christians are in a dilemma as to how to pray and for what to pray.

God has the answer by telling us that this is the ministry of the Holy Spirit. While the Lord Jesus was here, the disciples prayed, "Lord, teach us to pray" (Luke 11:1). Doesn't it follow, then, that Christians should seek and depend on the Holy Spirit to help and direct them in prayer? Go to the proper authority in this area as well. It could transform your prayer life. Paul admonishes us to pray "always with all prayer and supplication in the Spirit" (Eph. 6:18). Could this be the answer to the frustrations in your prayer life? Try the Holy Spirit in this area of Christian growth.

FULFILLING THE LAW

One inclusive ministry is given in Romans 8:4: "The righteousness of the law might be fulfilled in us, who walk not after the flesh, but after the Spirit." Every born-again person's heart longs for righteousness to be produced in his life. To go down the list of the Ten Commandments can be discouraging. It is thrilling, though, when one realizes that he himself cannot stop his coveting or other problems, and then begins to trust and expect the Holy Spirit to overcome them. You can be sure that, given the opportunity, the Holy Spirit will accomplish much more in a shorter time than all the struggling of the flesh for years before. It is not a passive permission but a definite, deliberate dependence on the Holy Spirit that brings the results.

WALK IN THE SPIRIT

"This I say then, Walk in the Spirit, and ye shall not fulfill the lust of the flesh" (Gal. 5:16). What a phenomenal promise. He did not say, "You won't have any desires of the flesh," but he said, "You won't *fulfill* the desires of the flesh." Some have erroneously taught that you will come to a place of losing all your urges and desires of sin. Often when some have felt they have come to such an experience, but then are again tempted to sin, they become totally disillusioned and defeated. No, I repeat, He said, "You won't *fulfill* the desires of the flesh." He did not say, "You won't have a desire to sin." There just has to be that conscious dependence on the Holy Spirit to see victory accomplished. Bless God, this promise will be fulfilled when one lets the Holy Spirit do what He came to do.

THE FRUIT OF THE SPIRIT

"But the fruit of the Spirit is love, joy, peace, long-suffering, gentleness, goodness, faith, meekness, temperance: against such there is no law" (Gal. 5:22, 23). These are not personality traits that some have and some don't. They are the beautiful fruit produced in abundance by the Holy Spirit when He controls a life. One does not shake a fruit tree or pull and twist its branches to make it produce. You just cultivate that tree and that is the way it produces the fruit. Christians need only to learn to cultivate their lives so that the Holy Spirit flows freely within to produce His fruit. There is no way in the world anyone can love those who are unlovely or enemies apart from a bushel of this fruit of love produced in his life.

THE LIBERTY OF THE SPIRIT

Spirit-filled preachers know wonderful liberty in preaching. The message just flows. There is no searching or stumbling for words. The people are really with you. Your message is coming through and you know it. Spirit-filled soul-winners know this liberty also. There is no striving. There is no fear. Witnessing just seems to be natural and easy. How does this come about? God says, "Where the Spirit of the Lord is, there is liberty" (2 Cor. 3:17). Oh, the pure delight in preaching and witnessing in that liberty!

What a difference there is in a church service when the Holy Spirit is not grieved or quenched and you sense the Holy Spirit is in total control. The singing lifts you, the service is alive. Announcements, offering, special music, all seem so different and a blessing. What a strain, though, when you don't sense this liberty. Nothing seems to go right. Everything is a struggle. What makes the difference? The Holy Spirit, and He alone produces this liberty.

TRANSFORMATION BY THE SPIRIT

One last thing, but perhaps one of the most important factors, is the transformation, the change, that the Holy Spirit produces. "But we all, with open face beholding as in a glass the glory of the Lord, are changed . . . from glory to glory even as by the Spirit" (2 Cor. 3:18). We have seen those who radiate Christ. Their faces beam. Joy bubbles from them. Love is genuinely poured through their lives. The simple truth is that they bear the image of Christ. God declares this change is "by the Spirit." When Moses came from the presence of God and his face glowed, the Bible says he knew "not that the skin of his face shone" (Exod. 34:29).

This deep, wonderful, genuine spirituality is God's doing. Man doesn't put it on like so much make-up. It just comes through from within. Bless God, it is available to all who will yield to the powerful and intricate work of the Holy Spirit. Christians need to be discerning, not divisive, about this. Believers need to quit struggling and striving to attain spirituality and simply let the Holy Spirit take over their lives to see all this accomplished in them.

Yes, the Savior finished what He came to do, then went to heaven and sat down. Now the Holy Spirit wants to take up where Christ left off and finish what God only started at the moment of salvation.

Study Questions: Chapter 2

1. Discuss the different ministries in each age of each Person in the Trinity.
2. What is the specific difference in the ministries of the Lord Jesus and the Holy Spirit in salvation?
3. Name and discuss the ministries of the Holy Spirit in believers today.
4. How does "Christ live in us" today?

3
How on Earth Can I Travel First Class?

Traveling first class is so much better than being in the often-crowded, cramped, uncomfortable economy section. The contrast is especially vivid on steamships going across the ocean. First-class quarters are larger, more plush. The food is so much better, and there is more of it. There are swimming pools, games of all kinds, the best deck for promenades, and deck chairs for relaxing and basking in the sun. None of these conveniences are for passengers traveling in the lower-class sections.

Too many Christians are not traveling first class on their way to heaven. The tragedy of life is not what men suffer, but what they miss! God has provided for *all* to travel first class with all the enjoyments of life along the way. "I am come that they might have life, and that they might have it more abundantly" (John 10:10). Oh, yes, every saved person will make it to heaven, but too many aren't enjoying the trip. They are just existing. They are missing the benefits available to them. What makes the difference? The Holy Spirit Himself. All of the extra comforts and luxuries are bound up in our relationship with Him.

God has even given us names for the first-class and the second-class Christians. In 1 Corinthians 2:14ff., God classifies individuals. First, He speaks of the "natural man" (v. 14). Then He talks about the "spiritual" man in verse 15, and the "carnal" Christian in 3:1. These three classes sum up all of mankind. The natural man is the unsaved man who has never been born again. The spiritual man is the Christian who is traveling first class to heaven. The carnal man is the Christian who is traveling second class to heaven.

THE ALIEN
About the natural man God says, "But the natural man

receiveth not the things of the Spirit of God: for they are foolishness unto him: neither can he know them, because they are spiritually discerned" (1 Cor. 2:14). The natural man is the person who has only been born naturally. He has never had the second birth, the supernatural birth. Jesus said, "Ye must be born again" (John 3:7). No one goes to heaven without this new birth and this citizenship. Without it one is simply a natural man and will die both the first death, the physical, and the second death, separation from God forever. He is not even going to heaven in the first place.

† = CHRIST
D = DEVIL
F = FLESH OF SELF

Figure 3.

Figure 3 illustrates the natural man and his heart. The cross, representing Christ, is on the outside. The natural man has never received the Lord Jesus into his heart as his own Savior. He is in the driver's seat of life, represented by "F" for the flesh. His motto is, "I am the captain of my ship; I am the master of my soul." Like those in Matthew 7:22, he one day will ask, "Lord, have we not prophesied in thy name? and in thy name have cast out devils? and in thy name done many wonderful works?" (Matt. 7:22). And then God will say, "I never knew you: depart from me, ye that work iniquity" (Matt. 7:23). The "Natural Man" will be startled and ask, "You mean we can't get into heaven after doing all of this?"

You see with his good works he is trying to drive right up to the gates of heaven. He, like so many today, will not believe God when He says that it is "not by works of right- eousness" (Titus 3:5) that He saves us, but simply "he that hath the Son hath life" (1 John 5:12). God says, "As many as received him [the Lord Jesus], to them gave he [the right]

to become the sons of God . . . which were born . . . of God"
(John 1:12,13). The natural man never had time for Christ
himself. He was in the driver's seat, trying to build up points
to get into heaven. Many think that every time they do a
good deed they get a green stamp, and if they can fill up
enough books they will make it to heaven.

Self, or the flesh, is in the driver's seat and all too much of
the flesh comes out, for "the works of the flesh are manifest,
which are these; Adultery, fornication, uncleanness, lasciviousness, idolatry, witchcraft, hatred, variance, emulations, wrath,
strife, seditions, heresies, envyings, murders, drunkenness,
revellings, and such like: of the which I tell you before, as I
have also told you in time past, that they which do such
things shall not inherit the kingdom of God" (Gal. 5:19-21).
All these deeds are signposts that ought to tell a person if he
is on his way to heaven or to hell.

Jesus said, "I am the way . . . no man cometh unto the
Father, but by me" (John 14:6). If all signs point toward
hell, you need to get on a new road. Christ is the Way. One
doesn't need to change his way of living to get to heaven.
That would be like changing the signposts. He needs to get
on a new road, going in a new direction; he needs to receive
the Lord Jesus. The signposts, his way of living, will be
changing, but it will be done from the inside by the Lord
Himself in the new birth.

This natural man has the devil, represented by the "D" (in
Figure 3), by his side prodding him along. In fact, God
says he is "taken captive by [Satan] at his will" (2 Tim. 2:26).
What a sad slavery. The only way to be delivered from
Satan, sin, and self is to receive the Lord Jesus into one's
heart.

But the natural man receives not the things of God; "they
are foolishness unto him" (1 Cor. 2:14). There is a door
made up of three panels—emotion, intellect, and will—leading to man's heart. Emotionally the natural man is unmoved,
untouched. His heart is hard and unresponsive. The suffering of the Lord Jesus on the cross for his sins means nothing.
Then 1 Corinthians 2:14 says, "Neither can he know them."

This is the intellectual panel. Though he hears the gospel or reads it, it just never makes sense. Stranger than fiction is how a man can accept by faith all the theories of evolution, with the hundreds of unknown and unproven aspects, and yet turn down the much more logical fact of a Creator who made it all! As Christians, we need to know the natural man cannot receive the truth apart from the Holy Spirit enlightening him. This drives us to depend on the Holy Spirit exclusively as we share the gospel.

The third panel of the door to the natural man's heart is his will: He "receiveth not the things of the Spirit of God." By deliberate choice the natural man "loves darkness rather than light, because his deeds are evil" (John 3:19). The final decision is left to a man's willingness to receive the Lord Jesus.

God still declares, "Whosoever *will,* let him take the water of life freely" (Rev. 22:17, italics mine). This alone will make him a citizen of heaven. This alone will put him on board and get him to heaven. Have you gotten on board yet? Why not bow your head and let God know you will receive the Lord Jesus right now? He will come into your heart as He promised. "Behold, I stand at the door, and knock: if any man hear my voice, and open the door, I will come in to him, and will sup with him, and he with me" (Rev. 3:20).

FIRST-CLASS CITIZENS

When one has received the Lord Jesus, the class in which he travels is then determined by his relationship to the Holy Spirit. The question remains, who is in the driver's seat? (See Figure 4.)

NATURAL   SPIRITUAL

Figure 4.

Now look at the second heart (Figure 4). Notice that the cross is inside. This person has received the Lord Jesus as his own Savior. See who is in the driver's seat: the Holy Spirit. God wants a man, after he has let the Savior convert him, to let the Spirit control him. The spiritual man is one who is controlled by the Holy Spirit.

Don't miss this. You don't become good to be saved. Good works won't produce salvation, but salvation will produce good works. Likewise, you don't become godly to become spiritual, you become spiritual to become godly. This statement is the key to this whole book. Read it again and again until you thoroughly understand it.

Figure 5.

Look at Figure 5. Many think a sinner starts to climb the road of good works and gets better and better until he reaches the stage of being saved. Then many a Christian carries this philosophy over into Christianity to feel he must climb the road higher and higher and get better and better until he reaches the stage of being a spiritual Christian.

But this is not true. The minute he asks the Holy Spirit to get in the driver's seat, He takes control and begins producing a spiritual life. There can be different amounts of spiritual fruit in each person's life, depending on how long he has been letting the Holy Spirit control him. He can be a baby Christian and be a Spirit-controlled baby Christian. Also, there is a difference in spirituality and spiritual maturity, which will be explained in chapter 12.

The spiritual man is traveling first class. He is enjoying the wonderful fruit of the Spirit: "love, joy, peace, long-suffering, gentleness, goodness, faith, meekness, temperance." His life is filled with joy, even though he is faced with tribulation and problems just as everyone else is (John 16:33). This first-class travel assures one of a life of peace—not only peace *with* God but the peace *of* God. This Christian is not immunized from the pressures of life nor from problems, but he knows "all things work together for good to them that . . . are the called [of God]" (Rom. 8:28).

And he can rest in perfect peace while a storm rages all around! He has a purpose in life. He knows where he is going. God directs the affairs of his life, and he travels in style as the Holy Spirit controls. This traveler doesn't blow a gasket or lose his cool but has the power and the peace of God to be able to take the bumps of life. Life is so fulfilling and rewarding, for he has "found himself" and God's purpose for life. He isn't a fish out of water. Life is wonderful.

Notice the Lord Jesus is exalted in the Christian's life by the Holy Spirit. "He shall glorify me" (John 16:14). Anyone who claims to have the truth must be exalting Christ above all. There is a lot of talk about making Jesus Lord of our lives. God declares, "No man can say that Jesus is the Lord, but by the Holy Ghost" (1 Cor. 12:3). When one travels first class with the Holy Spirit in the driver's seat, he makes Christ Lord of his life and through his life. You just don't make Christ Savior or Lord through any human effort but by the power and control of the Holy Spirit. The sooner a Christian understands that the spiritual Christian life is "not by works" too, the sooner he is going to experience this transforming power in his life.

Here is one sure criterion of what to determine if a particular person or group is of God or not. Just ask yourself, "How much do they make of the Lord Jesus? Is He preeminent?" If some other doctrine or person is exalted, look out.

SECOND-CLASS CITIZENS

Look now at the carnal Christian, or the one *traveling second class*. (See Figure 6.) He is a citizen of heaven. He has Christ, but Christ is not lifted up in his life. The Lord

Figure 6.

Jesus is not exalted. There is very little praise of the Lord Jesus.

This is a worldly Christian. He loves the things of the world. He can fit right in. Worldly amusements and worldly habits occupy his time and tastes. He does these things because he is carnal; they don't make him become carnal. His affections are not on things above (Col. 3:1). He is laying up treasures on earth and not in heaven (Matt. 6:19). He is enjoying the pleasures of sin for a season (Heb. 11:25). His life is a tragic waste. His life is like a sixteen-cylinder Cadillac running on two cylinders!

In the end he will see all of his works go up in smoke, and he will suffer great loss of reward (1 Cor. 3:11ff.). Because of his life, often the Word of God is blasphemed (Titus 2:5). These will be ashamed before the Lord at His coming (1 John 2:28), and the Son of man shall be ashamed of them as well (Luke 9:26).

What makes him a carnal Christian? The word "carnal" means "flesh" or "self." This man has let the flesh, or self, get in the driver's seat again. He has grabbed the wheel and is trying to run his own life.

You then see the works of the flesh being produced. He loses his patience. His temper flares up. Jealousy is aroused. Hate creeps in. Lust crops out. A love for things of this world is renewed. Worldliness characterizes his life once more. He begins to conform to this world.

A worldly Christian is worldly because he is carnal; he does not become carnal because he is worldly. This is important to understand. Once again the age-old question comes up: Which comes first, the hen or the egg? In this case being carnal comes first, and then the works of the flesh are produced. This seems obvious, but it really is not recognized by most people. There is a serious danger of trying to cut off the works of the flesh by sheer struggle and human effort instead of turning over the control of our lives to the Holy Spirit. Reread this statement, for it is the key to restored joy and power in one's life.

A carnal Christian can have all the signs of a natural man. His highway signs can read just like the signs of the one on his way to hell. How can one determine if a person is just a carnal Christian or still unsaved, having never been born again? Two things seem to be evident from Scripture: conviction and chastening. If a person has been born again, the Holy Spirit lives within and is grieved. The Holy Spirit is faithful and "will convict of sin." The carnal man will lack the fruit of the Spirit: love, joy, peace. He, like David, will not have the joy of his salvation (Ps. 51:12). Like David also, his sin will be ever before him (Ps. 51:3).

Second, the carnal man will be chastened of the Lord. If a person *claims* to be saved and yet the works of the flesh are manifested in his life and he is never chastened by God, God declares that that one is not saved (Heb. 12:8). He is deceiving himself; he needs a checkup. Weakness, sickness, and even death will come to a Christian who walks in the flesh (1 Cor. 11:30). We know from Scripture that Satan blinds the minds of the unsaved world (2 Cor. 4:4). Multitudes attend church regularly who have never had a real checkup. All through the week nothing but the flesh is evident, and they never consider this to be a sign that they have never been born again.

If you are truly born again, then act like it. If the works of the flesh are being manifest, recognize your condition to be that of a carnal man. Don't begin by reforming and trying harder; begin by picturing who is in the driver's seat. Slide out from behind the wheel and ask the Holy Spirit to take over the control of your life once again. There and then alone will the real fruit of the Spirit—love, joy, peace—be produced, and it will be really sweet.

Study Questions: Chapter 3

1. Describe the natural man.
2. Discuss the place of good works in relation to salvation.
3. What is a carnal man, and what are his traits?
4. How can a person determine if he is just a carnal Christian or has never really been born again?
5. Discuss the spiritual man and first-class living.
6. What is the real difference between a carnal and a spiritual Christian?

4
How on Earth Can I Be Filled With the Holy Spirit?

"Be filled with the Spirit" (Eph. 5:18). What potential there is in being filled with the Holy Spirit. It turned stumbling Peter into a stunning preacher (Acts 4:8ff.). What power there is in this! Being filled with the Holy Spirit, Peter preached, and three thousand people were smitten in their hearts and converted in one day (Acts 2). What is the purpose in being filled? Because the early Christians were filled with joy, they lived in one accord and witnessed with boldness (Acts 4:31ff.).

Does being filled with the Holy Spirit sound like a panacea? Well, it is. Does it sound like a cure-all for the church? It most surely is. Does it sound like the answer to the needs of believers today? Make no mistake, it is. Does it sound like what your heart longs for? Then read on. It has transformed untold millions when being filled with the Spirit became a reality and not just some oft-repeated religious term in the Bible.

"Be ye not unwise, but understanding what the will of the Lord is. And be not drunk with wine, wherein is excess; but be filled with the Spirit" (Eph. 5:17,18). God often declares, "Be not ignorant." He wants us to "understand." A subtle device of Satan is to keep Christians in the dark with the idea that one can't "understand" so many spiritual things. To most believers, how to be filled with the Holy Spirit is just a fantasy and a mystery. Many take a fatalistic attitude that the power and filling of the Holy Spirit is for some select few and not attainable for all. The simple fact is that God wants us to understand, and He will give understanding if anyone really wants to know the truth (John 7:17).

UNDERSTANDING MUST COME FIRST

God declares the reason a man is not saved is that he doesn't *understand* the Word of God that he receives from the sower. The sower sows the seed, which is the Word of God (Luke 8:11). The seed is sown in a person's heart (Matt. 13:19). Some seed falls by the wayside or on stony ground or among thorns. This describes how it is when someone hears the Word of God but "understandeth it not" (Matt. 13:19). He, therefore, is not saved, and Satan "catcheth away that which was sown in his heart."

"But he that received seed into the good ground is he that heareth the word, and *understandeth* it; which also beareth fruit, and bringeth forth, some an hundredfold, some sixty, some thirty" (Matt. 13:23, italics mine). The secret, then, of getting people saved is to give them the gospel, which "is the power of God unto salvation" (Rom. 1:16), until they *understand* the gospel and the basis on which God saves. Then they can believe and trust the finished work of Christ and let Him save them and give them life.

Now the parallel is for Christians to understand the will of God and *how* to have life more abundantly (John 10:10). What is the will of God? In decisions, no one but you can know what the will of God is for your life. In decisions, you yourself may not be sure of the will of God. Here, though, is something every believer can be absolutely sure is the will of God, for God tells us to understand the will of God (Eph. 5:17).

First, "be not drunk with wine." Is it a sin to be drunk? Of course it is. No need to debate the issue or question it one minute. This is a command! Don't be drunk with wine! Second, in the same breath God says, "But be filled with the Spirit." Simple logic says that if it is a sin to be drunk with wine, then it is a sin not to be filled with the Spirit. Being filled with the Spirit is not optional, it is imperative. It is not something just for preachers or evangelists to experience; it is for all. The power and filling of the Holy Spirit is not needed just for preaching the gospel; it is essential for living the Christian life.

WHAT DOES "SPIRIT-FILLED" MEAN?

What does it mean to be filled with the Holy Spirit? Does it mean to get more and more of the Holy Spirit, like filling a glass with more and more water until it overflows? Some believe that. No, it isn't that at all, for the Holy Spirit is a person and you have all of Him the moment you are saved. You don't get Him piecemeal. To be filled with the Holy Spirit means to be *controlled by* the Holy Spirit. This is it. The secret to the Christian life is being controlled by the Holy Spirit so that He can produce in and through the believer all that is His ministry today

Notice carefully the comparison of being under the influence of alcohol or under the influence of the Holy Spirit. God says don't be drunk with wine, don't be under the control of alcohol, but be filled with the Spirit, be under the control of the Holy Spirit. The late Dr. Kenneth Wuest, a great Greek scholar, once said, "Being filled with the Holy Spirit is not putting gas in the tank; it is putting a Driver at the wheel." That's it. Who is in the driver's seat of your life? Who is in control of your life?

Figure 7.

As Figure 7 shows, a Christian is one who has Christ in his heart, as represented by the cross. A Spirit-controlled Christian is one who has gotten himself, the flesh, out from behind the wheel and allowed the Holy Spirit to get in the driver's seat and run his life. Later in this chapter we will go into detail as to how to let the Holy Spirit get in the driver's seat.

There is a vast difference between the two concepts. There has been much confusion among sincere people because this distinction has not been made. As long as one is "being filled" or "controlled" by the Holy Spirit, he will see "the fruit of the Spirit" being produced and will be "temperate" or "self-controlled," as the word means (Gal. 5:22,23). This is the work of the Spirit and not the result of will power. The only means of self-control is the Holy Spirit controlling the flesh and its desires.

A Christian must be aware that this is a continuous yielding to the control of the Holy Spirit. The minute the flesh gets in the driver's seat, the Holy Spirit moves from the *controlling* ministry to the *convicting* ministry. That Christian then loses the joy of the Lord, which is the fruit of the Spirit, and begins feeling miserable. He doesn't lose his salvation, only the joy of his salvation (Ps. 51:12). All truth fits if we will only "rightly [divide] the word of truth" (2 Tim. 2:15).

The statement "be filled" is in the imperative mood in the original language, which means it is a *command*. It is not optional, nor is it simply suggestive. This puts force behind it to say emphatically again: It is a sin not to be a Spirit-filled or controlled Christian. Another fact brought out in the original language is that this statement is in the present progressive tense, which means "be ye *continually* filled" with the Spirit. Letting the Savior convert you is a once-for-all act, but letting the Spirit control you is a moment-by-moment continuous act. This is very important.

Being filled is not one single dramatic act which transforms you into some super-Christian or translates you into a realm of super-spirituality above all others. You do not suddenly become "sanctified wholly," never to sin again. The old desires to sin don't leave you, never to return. You are simply under the control or power of the Holy Spirit as long as you keep your hands off the wheel. God said you will not *fulfill* the desires of the flesh, not that you won't *have* any desires of the flesh, as you walk in dependence on the Holy Spirit.

Have you ever noticed the parallels of being drunk with wine and being filled with the Holy Spirit? They did on the day of Pentecost and accused those "filled with the Holy Spirit" of being "full of new wine" (Acts 2:13). Peter corrected them and said, "These are not drunken, as ye suppose, seeing it is but the third hour of the day. But this is that which was spoken by the prophet Joel; and it shall come to pass in the last days, saith God, I will pour out of my Spirit upon all flesh" (Acts 2:15-17).

There are some great lessons to be learned by noting the parallels. Have you ever noticed how someone who is drunk will love everybody, even strangers? A Spirit-controlled Christian will love people, even the lost, for "the love of God is shed abroad in our hearts by the Holy Ghost" (Rom. 5:5).

When a person gets drunk, his tongue gets loose. He will talk the brass horns off a billy goat. A Christian filled with the Holy Spirit will have his tongue loosed, and he will witness, for God declares, "Ye shall receive power, after that the Holy Ghost is come upon you: and ye shall be witnesses unto me" (Acts 1:8). He didn't say you *might* witness; He said emphatically: "Ye *shall be* witnesses." Look at it as a great promise and provision.

Another parallel is the boldness each has. A drunk will pick a fight with a much larger man and not have a bit of fear. A Spirit-filled Christian has a boldness not possible in the flesh, as witnessed in Acts 4:31, "And when they had prayed, the place was shaken where they were assembled together; and they were all filled with the Holy Ghost, and they spake the word of God with boldness." Many a fearful saint needs to know this provision and appropriate it, for "God hath not given us the spirit of fear; but of power, and of love, and of a sound mind" (2 Tim. 1:7).

Along with this, note that a drunk is totally uninhibited. He loses all self-consciousness. Spirit-controlled Christians do the same; they are uninhibited. Someone has said self-consciousness is sin. Indeed, one who is self-conscious surely is not consciously depending on the Holy Spirit, is he? We are commanded to be filled with, to depend on, the Holy Spirit. This is strong medicine. This is not milk but meat of the Word. This separates the men from the boys. Christians need to rid themselves of all their alibis and appropriate the power and provision of the Holy Spirit.

Drunks become generous. They will spend their last dime to buy someone else a drink and cry to the bartender, "Set 'em up." Spirit-filled Christians of the early church were certainly generous, for they sold all their possessions and gave the money to the apostles to be given to all who had a need (Acts 4:32-37). Wouldn't that impress the lost world today?

A drunk person likes to be around other drunks. Spirit-filled Christians certainly like to be around others who are spiritual. They just don't have an appetite to sit at home and watch TV on Sunday night any more than a drunk wants to go to church on Sunday night. God says believers are not to forsake the assembling of themselves (Heb. 10:25). Those Spirit-filled Christians kept company with each other. "And they, continuing daily in one accord in the temple, and breaking bread from house to house, did eat their meat with gladness and singleness of heart, praising God, and having favor with all the people" (Acts 2:46,47). These people are to be envied and emulated. They certainly aren't to be pitied, for there was an awful lot of love and joy among them.

Why not get in on it? If you aren't experiencing these blessings in your own life, it's your own fault. Don't rationalize and explain away your own symptoms. Get mad at the devil for robbing you of this Spirit-controlled life, and then begin letting the Holy Spirit produce the fruit in you.

WHO IS THE HOLY SPIRIT?

If we are to be controlled by the Holy Spirit, we need to know more about the Holy Spirit than the average Christian seems to know. Notice the personal pronouns in John 16:13, 14: "Howbeit when *he,* the Spirit of truth, is come, *he* will guide you into all truth: for *he* shall not speak of *himself;* but whatsoever *he* shall hear, that shall *he* speak: and *he* will shew you things to come. *He* shall glorify me: for *he* shall receive of mine, and shall shew it unto you" (italics mine).

Who in the world is the Holy Spirit? Why, He is a wonderful *Person.* He is not an "it." The statement, "You'll know *it* when *it* hits you," is an erroneous way to talk about the Holy

Spirit. He's a Person. He is not an influence. At Christmastime people speak of the spirit of Christmas. They mean that good feeling people experience. The Holy Spirit is not some vague feeling. He is a Person. He is just as real as the Lord Jesus. He has emotion, intellect, and will, just as any other being. All the eternal attributes of God the Father are His. It is so important to recognize Him as a real Person, though He is a Spirit.

WHERE IS THE HOLY SPIRIT?

Where in the world is the Holy Spirit? Notice the question asks where "in the world." He is in the world today, though unseen by human eyes (John 14:17). The Christians of Paul's day didn't know where He was, so Paul said, "What? know ye not that your body is the Temple of the Holy Ghost which is in you, which ye have of God, and ye are not your own? For ye are bought with a price: therefore glorify God in your body, and in your spirit, which are God's (1 Cor. 6:19, 20). Where is the Holy Spirit? He is in your body. Your body is the temple of the Holy Spirit.

There is a song that has had great influence upon the church's thinking. Often on Sunday morning the choir members come out in their beautiful robes. The organist plays softly. Everyone sits up straight and polishes his halo as the choir intones, "The Lord is in His holy temple; let all the earth be silent."

What a transformation can take place when one realizes his body is the temple of the Holy Spirit. He can get up on Monday morning and sing, "The Lord is in His holy temple; let all the world shut up!" He can beat upon his breast and say joyously, "Here's the temple of God. The Holy Spirit is in His holy temple." What an astounding thought! This makes a Christian's body ever so important. It will make a world of difference how one treats this body, what enters this body, and where one goes in this body, when this truth is fully realized.

Roman Catholics reverently make a sign when they enter their churches; they cross themselves. There is a sign made by thousands of others before they enter their church: They stand outside "fellowshipping," and just before they enter they take one last puff and flip with their finger and send the cigarette flying. Oh, they wouldn't think of smoking in the house of God. What a difference it makes when one realizes his body is the temple of God. The Holy Spirit lives inside. If it's wrong to smoke in the church, then doesn't it make sense to say it's wrong to fill your body, the temple of the Holy Spirit, with smoke?

Smoking is not the only thing that defiles the body. Drinking, drugs, overeating, and underexercising, as well as many other things, can harm the temple of God. It is a tragedy to see so many Christians eat like pigs until they are just plain fat and slothful. Certainly gluttony is a sin. God says strongly, "Put a knife to thy throat, if thou be a man given to appetite" (Prov. 23:2). Husbands and wives often lose their attractiveness to each other by allowing themselves to be obese and then wonder what happened to their romance!

A church where I preached one Sunday was unusually cold, unfriendly, and unresponsive. Later that day they had a potluck dinner at the church. During that meal I suddenly became aware of the fact that an unusual number were just plain fat. I watched as they piled their plates and gorged themselves. Frankly, I lost my appetite. I sincerely believe the sin of gluttony had a grip on that church and was affecting the working of the Holy Spirit in a marked way. Never have I seen such a sight in any other church to the degree it was evidenced there.

No one likes to come home to a dirty, untidy house. A man would hate to have to kick trash out of his path to get to the kitchen. It would be repulsive to eat off a dirty table and dirty plates or to drink from a filthy glass. How much more does the Holy Spirit feel uncomfortable to live in a Christian if that Christian's life is full of sin. This certainly grieves the Holy Spirit. He then ceases to work *through* that person and begins to work *on* him in conviction.

Often I have been a weekend guest in a house when I'm speaking at meetings. One weekend in a dramatic way a truth was illustrated in one of those homes. As the husband brought me to his house, his wife met us at the door in the hallway. It was obvious those dear people had not entertained preachers before and were ill at ease. They stood in the hallway awkwardly talking, even though it was below zero outside and cold in the hallway. Suddenly, the wife nervously said, "John, take Brother Wemp upstairs to his room." And he said, "Oh, yes, come on, Brother Wemp." We went up, he opened the door, pointed in, and said, also nervously, "Here's your room, Brother Wemp." I felt he was saying, "and stay there; we don't know what to do with you." They were obviously unused to having company. I felt uneasy there and rather shut up in the room.

It then dawned on me: This is the way many feel about the Holy Spirit. They think of Him as a guest shut up in the guest room until church time. He wants to feel at home and have access to every room of our lives.

WHY DOES THE HOLY SPIRIT LIVE IN ME?

You may ask, "Why in the world does the Holy Spirit live in my body?" He says He wants to fill our house and control everything, as though our house is a factory. He wants to run the factory and be allowed to produce vast quantities of His fruit—love, joy, peace.

He wants also to produce temperance or "self-control." Self-control might be better thought of as control of the flesh. This flesh is by nature in opposition to the Holy Spirit and opposed to doing the will of God. It must be brought under control. The Holy Spirit is the only One who can control it. But, bless God, He *can* control it until He brings "into captivity every thought to the obedience of Christ" (2 Cor. 10:5). This is real victory. The Holy Spirit alone can accomplish this.

HOW CAN I BE SPIRIT-FILLED?

You may ask, "How in the world can I be filled with the Holy Spirit?" The simple "how to" is so easy, yet so elusive. Just as Satan is a master at deception to keep non-Christians from understanding and accepting the simplicity of conversion or salvation, so he is a master of keeping Christians from understanding and accepting the simplicity of control or Spirit-filled living.

The key verses to making this a reality are 1 John 5:14,15: "And this is the confidence that we have in him, that, if we ask any thing according to his will, he heareth us: and if we know that he hear us, whatsoever we ask, we know that we have the petitions that we desired of him." John says this is the confidence that we as Christians have in God. We are confident, absolutely sure, that if we ask anything according to the will of God we will *have it!* The important thing in asking is to be sure it is the *"will of God."*

Two of our children have been afflicted with illnesses for which doctors have told us there is no cure. For both of them we have prayed earnestly. Our first child was ill for seven years, and God wondrously healed him. For over twenty years he has taken no medicine, nor has he had one recurrence of his illness. To God be the glory! We found out about our other child and her illness some fifteen years later. We have prayed earnestly for four years, but God has not yet healed her.

What a blessing both illnesses have been. In it all we have given thanks and have nothing but praise to God, for we know "all things work together for good to them that love God" (Rom. 8:28). You see, we just don't know with absolute certainty about God's will in these matters. So we have to pray with the ultimate goal of "not my will, but thine, be done" (Luke 22:42). This has to be kept in mind in our prayer lives, unless we know from the Word of God that what we pray for is the will of God.

Here, now, is the key to being controlled by the Holy Spirit. Ephesians 5:17 tells us emphatically to understand that to be filled with the Holy Spirit *is the will of God.* That means that if I ask for the Holy Spirit to fill me, to take control, He does! We *know* we have this petition (1 John 5:15, italics mine). How do we know? By feeling joy or a warm love oozing through us? No. We know by *faith* that God cannot lie, and so we live by faith. We walk by faith. We trust that at the moment we ask He gets behind the wheel and begins to take control. In the following days as He controls, we will see the fruit being produced. It will then be a fantastic experience to see the changes take place that He brings about. What's so amazing, and surprises even the believer, is that he finds himself loving people in a way so different from how he has in the past. He then is aware that God did it, and it was not the struggle of the flesh and his own efforts that brought it about.

The week after I was saved God gave me a fantastic evidence that He had saved me. Before I became a Christian, I had a terrible temper and tongue. One day I was driving a nail with a hammer. Suddenly I hit the wrong nail—the one on my thumb—as hard as I had ever hit my finger. When I did, I let out the word "Ouch!" Suddenly I realized I had not done the thing which I normally would have done—that is, curse. I broke into tears, bowed my head, and thanked God He had saved me and already let me see a dramatic change in my life. To God be the glory, I have never said one word of profanity since the day I was saved.

Often just as dramatically, a Christian will see even greater changes in his life day by day as he begins consciously to ask the Holy Spirit to control him. He must ask Him by faith and then wait and expect to see the results in the days that follow.

There is another significant verse that can be used as a guide to know this control of the Holy Spirit. Paul exhorts, "I beseech you therefore, brethren, by the mercies of God, that ye present your bodies a living sacrifice, holy, acceptable unto God, which is your reasonable service" (Rom. 12:1). Your body is the temple of the Holy Spirit. God wants a Christian to present that body as a *living* sacrifice, given up to the control of the Holy Spirit.

Another wonderful fact is brought out in the original language in this verse. In the Greek the tense of the word "present" speaks of the initial act. Sometimes this initial act can be dramatic in the Christian's life. There can be a great amount of emotion involved. As with the initial act of salvation, the reaction is different with each individual. One should not judge his experience by another person's nor try to duplicate another's experience. Neither should one demand nor expect that another have the same outward response as he to be convinced that that person has really presented his body and is now a Spirit-filled Christian. There is absolutely no outward criterion that is a proof one has had this experience of being filled.

Another term that God uses to explain a relationship with the Holy Spirit is *yield*. He says, "Yield yourselves unto God, as those that are alive from the dead, and your members as instruments of righteousness unto God" (Rom. 6:13). Here the idea is to give up the control of one's life. The Holy Spirit moves and strives to gain control. A Christian is not to quench the Holy Spirit but simply live yielded to the Holy Spirit. An acrostic is helpful in remembering this key truth: PAY—Present, Ask, and Yield.

It matters not what term or method you use to allow the Holy Spirit to be in the driver's seat as long as you consciously have Him in control. How do the vast majority of people finalize the act of receiving Christ as Savior? By praying. God says, "Whosoever shall call upon the Lord shall be saved" (Rom. 10:13). This act of praying and asking the Lord Jesus to come into one's heart seems to be the most assuring and the simplest method of getting saved.

Does one have to pray to be saved? Not actually. On several occasions I have seen people saved before my eyes as they believed on the Lord Jesus in their hearts without any specific act of praying, but prayer is the most common way of settling it. So with becoming filled or controlled by the Holy Spirit, praying and asking for Him to take control or get into the driver's seat is the most common way for most people.

A startling fact has come to me as I have preached hundreds of times: It is about as hard to get Christians to let the Holy Spirit control them as it is to get non-Christians to let the Savior convert them. Think this through. A non-Christian will use the excuse, "I don't feel ready." A soul-winner will plead, "Don't depend on feelings. There is no particular feeling that says this is it. Christ is to be accepted by faith." So it is with letting the Holy Spirit control you.

Again, a non-Christian will make the excuse, "I don't know if I can make the change or live up to it." To this the reply would be, "If you let the Savior save you, it is His responsibility to make the change, not yours." So, with becoming a Spirit-filled Christian, don't say, "I don't know if I can live it." The Holy Spirit is the One who causes the Spirit-filled living to be a reality. A non-Christian needs to let the Savior save him by faith, and a Christian needs to let the Spirit control him by faith.

Will you bow your head right now and, on the promise of 1 John 5:14,15, ask God for the Holy Spirit to take control of your life? How you feel has nothing to do with the fact. Your willingness to trust God to do what He promised is all that is needed. After you ask for the Holy Spirit to take control, then by faith know that He has done it and thank Him that right now you too are a Spirit-filled Christian. The glory of it all is that it works. God always keeps His promise when we meet the conditions and act upon His promise.

Someone said of D. L. Moody, "He has a monopoly on the Holy Spirit." Another replied, "No, the Holy Spirit has a monopoly on Mr. Moody." May this be true of you and me today.

Study Questions: Chapter 4

1. Is it the will of God for every Christian to be filled with the Holy Spirit?
2. What does it mean to be filled with the Holy Spirit?
3. Discuss the comparison of being drunk with wine and being filled with the Holy Spirit.
4. Discuss the differences between the convicting and controlling ministries of the Holy Spirit in the Christian's life.
5. Who is the Holy Spirit?
6. Where is the Holy Spirit today?
7. How is a believer to be filled with the Holy Spirit?

5
How on Earth Can I Walk In the Spirit?

The Christian is to walk with God (Gen. 6:9). That's his purpose. He is to walk after Christ (Matt. 4:19,20). That's his pattern. Finally, he is to "walk in the Spirit" (Gal. 5:16). That's his power. Over and over the Christian life is described as walking. One is to "walk in love" (Eph. 5:2), "walk circumspectly" (5:15), "walk as children of light" (5:8), "walk not as other Gentiles" (4:17), "walk worthy of the vocation wherewith ye are called" (4:1), as well as many other admonitions.

There is a danger of trying to "run the race" without learning to walk. That first step a child takes doesn't mean he has learned to walk yet. It takes time to learn to walk. A child will take a couple of steps and fall down and cry, but he must get up and go again. The Christian life is a walk, not one giant step. Many go to one conference after another looking for one big moment or experience, thinking they will then have it made. No, there isn't one giant step that gets you above sin or into victory-land with no more battles. In fact the more you walk in the Spirit, the more it terrifies Satan, and he will fire every fiery dart he can at you. But, bless God, you can quench every one of them and know victory as you "walk in the Spirit."

ENDING THE SPIRITUAL UPS AND DOWNS

Are you on the spiritual roller coaster, up one minute and down the next? (See Figure 8.) Probably most Christians live their entire Christian lives like this. When they come to Christ, they are on a spiritual high. They have that "first love" and couldn't be any happier. They read their Bibles all the time. The church doors aren't open enough; they want to go all the time. They are excited about the Lord.

Then they get cooled off as they watch the more mature Christians and hear their gripes and gossip. One thing leads to another until suddenly they find themselves discouraged and defeated. They hit bottom. Oh, this doesn't mean they have gone back to the old life of drinking and cursing, but the Christian life is now blah. Their heart just isn't in it. Along comes a week of special meetings and they "rededicate their lives," and they are back on top again. That cycle gets repeated year after year. This should not be the normal life.

The normal Christian life should look more like the bottom example in Figure 8. Rather than big dips and hitting the

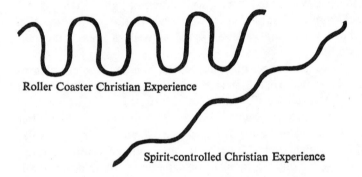

Roller Coaster Christian Experience

Spirit-controlled Christian Experience

Figure 8.

skids until they end up at the bottom, there should be just slight dips as they grow in the grace and knowledge of Christ. This life leads to higher levels of spiritual maturity day by day. It can be filled with joy as one walks in the Spirit. There will be times of stumbling, but taking the proper steps will keep one off the roller coaster and away from the valleys of deep depression and defeat. Let's see how this is accomplished in a practical way.

Depend on the Spirit

God says, "Walk in the Spirit." The word "in" and the case that follows has the distinct idea of walking in *dependence on* the Spirit. This is the secret. One is to depend on the Holy Spirit to do what He came to do—control him and produce in and through him all that the Word of God declares He will do. A Christian must realize that all the traits of spirituality are not attained by determination or degrees of effort, but by dependence on the Holy Spirit to produce them in him. It is not just a passive acquiescence to the Holy Spirit but an active dependency on and response to the Holy Spirit.

Walking in the Spirit must also be a *conscious* dependence. It is not a subconscious nor an unconscious dependence but a conscious and calculated dependence. What a difference there is in this fact. Many non-Christians will say glibly, "Oh, yes, I believe in the Lord Jesus." Yet there is no conscious dependence on Him as Savior. Most Christians will say, "Oh, yes, I believe in the Holy Spirit. I know that without the Lord I can do nothing." But there just is not a deliberate, conscious dependence on the Holy Spirit to accomplish in their lives what He says He will do. Because of this, there is no evidence of the power and fruit of the Holy Spirit. This conscious dependence on the Holy Spirit cannot be stressed too strongly, for here is the real reason so many people don't experience its reality. You cannot be passive about it.

The promise is, "Ye shall not fulfil the lust of the flesh" (Gal. 5:16). As was pointed out earlier, God did not say you won't *have* any lust or desires of the flesh. No. He said you won't fulfil or respond to the desires of the flesh.

The word "lust" in its initial sense means simply "desires." Now, contrary to some teaching, a Christian never loses all desire to sin. There is no experience this side of death whereby the old sin nature, the seat of sinful desires, is eradicated or removed. (More on this later in chapter 10.) There have been many shipwrecks along the way in Christians' lives because they had some dramatic experience in which they thought all desires to sin were gone. When temptations still came and desires were aroused, they became disillusioned and wondered what had happened.

Temptation is not sin. It is the yielding to temptation, the fulfilling of that desire, that is sin. How important it is to be discerning as to exactly what God said, and not add to or read into a passage something God never said nor meant. The promise not to fulfill the desires of the flesh is great enough. One must not seek the removal of all desires, of all temptation—of the old nature, if you please. God has made all the provision one needs. One just needs to appropriate the provision.

When a person does not consciously depend on the Holy Spirit, the old flesh, self, is standing by waiting for the chance to get in the driver's seat again. At that moment he is a carnal Christian. He is walking in the flesh, under the control of the flesh. The works of the flesh will be produced. Oh, Satan is wise; he does not tempt that carnal Christian into the depth of sin at that moment. Usually even a carnal Christian would be repulsed to go to the very bottom in sin. The progress downhill is usually little by little, step by step, as in the classic example of Lot in Genesis. It comes gradually.

Instead, we are to have a *constant,* conscious dependence on the Holy Spirit. As was pointed out, Ephesians 5:18 says, "Be filled," or "Be ye continuously controlled," by the Holy Spirit. It is not a once-for-all act, as in the case of the Savior saving a person. A Christian never "arrives." One cannot shift into overdrive, as it were, and have spirit-control become automatic in his life. There has to be that continuous dependence on the Holy Spirit.

Walking involves two steps—the right foot, then the left foot. So walking in the Spirit involves two steps. The one step is that of asking or allowing the Holy Spirit to take control. Before that can take place, though, often there is the need of another step. When a Christian becomes carnal and the flesh takes over again, there is the need of another step. That step is to confess sin.

Judge Yourself—Then Confess

A great Christian exercise that is terribly neglected is to "judge oneself." God says, "If we would judge ourselves, we should not be judged. But when we are judged, we are chastened of the Lord, that we should not be condemned with the world" (1 Cor. 11:31,32). Christians are to examine the fruit being produced in their lives to see if it is the fruit of the Spirit or the works of the flesh. This demands honesty with oneself. It also means knowing what the works of the flesh are, as described in Galatians 5:19-21. Even a Christian can rationalize until he hardly calls anything sin. One will need to sit in sincere judgment of himself in the light of the Word of God. Here is a list of deeds that need to be called what they are—the works of the flesh, and therefore sin.

Of course, there should be no questions about "adultery, fornication, uncleanness, and lasciviousness" being sin, to be confessed as such. "Idolatry" is sin, whether one sets up idols in his heart as described in Ezekiel 14 or in images. This would seem to indicate that anything that comes between a Christian and God is an idol. "Witchcraft" or sorcery is definitely of the flesh. It is astounding how many do not realize this includes all forms of fortune-telling and horoscopes. Also, far too many stay defeated and do not judge themselves in the matter of "sins of the spirit," such as hatred, strife, jealousy, wrath, factions, seditions, heresies, and envy.

When one harbors hatred of someone and yet says, "I love God," that one, God says, is a liar (1 John 4:20). To "strive" —get in arguments—is sin. Quarreling in homes must be judged and confessed. Jealousy is so deceptive. God surely knew what He was saying when He said, "Rejoice with them that do rejoice" (Rom. 12:15). Not to be able to do this indicates a measure of jealousy and therefore is sin. If he does not confess, the Christian invites chastening.

Wrath is declared sin and must be confessed. God says, "Let not the sun go down upon your wrath." This means deal with it, confess it, and make things right before one goes to bed. Many a man has wondered why his wife cannot respond to his needs at night. Often he has vented his wrath on her during the day without one word of apology. She goes to bed with a wounded spirit. "A wounded spirit who can bear?" says the wise man of Proverbs 18:14. If he would only live scripturally, judge himself, confess his sin, apologize to his wife and be reconciled, as Matthew 5:23,24 says, his wife could respond. This, of course, works for both parties of a marriage.

Then God names "strife," or "divisions," which the word really means. Splits and division in churches, until there are two factions pulling in different directions, means the flesh has taken over. Revivals could break out if Christians would judge themselves, and not someone else, to be wrong! Envy is designated a work of the flesh. Learning to "be content with such things as ye have" is a good remedy for envy. Murder and drunkenness and revelings should not be disputed as sin.

These all must be admitted to be sin. Then they must be confessed to the Lord to receive forgiveness. How hard it is for a Christian walking in the flesh to admit he is wrong. This, though, is what judging oneself means. This is the pathway to victory. Here is step number one to a continuous walk with God in the Spirit. "If we walk in the light" means examining our every deed and motive in the true light of the Word of God. We then will "have fellowship one with another, and the blood of Jesus Christ his Son cleanseth us from all sin" as we confess those sins (1 John 1:7–9).

Now comes that second step of asking for the Holy Spirit to take control again! All that Luke 11:13 means may not be clear, but it does indicate it is right to ask for the Holy Spirit. A Christian already possesses the Holy Spirit and cannot possess more of Him; but, through asking, the Holy Spirit can possess more of a Christian. This certainly is one indication of the verse! This must be done over and over.

A word of explanation about confessing sins might help at this point. The word *confess* in the Greek has at least two ideas inherent in it. One means "to agree with" God that the deed is sin and wrong. Don't quibble with God. Call it what it is. The late Dr. William Culbertson, when president of Moody Bible Institute, used to say so often, "Have no controversy with God."

Then there is also the idea of naming it. It is quite easy to try to tone down confession and gloss over confronting sin as it should be by praying the vague prayer of asking God to "forgive us of all our sins!" This is a cop-out! He says confess them, and I will (see 1 John 1:9). Some reading this perhaps have never had the burden lifted because they haven't admitted a particular sin to God. There remains a barrier in many hearts because they have not named their sin to God. The freedom from guilt and the liberty of true fellowship with God is lacking because some have not been sincerely honest with God and called the sin by name. A flood of joy and peace could come if that sin were genuinely confessed.

One other course of action often needs to be taken, and that is an apology. Private sin should be kept private. Once a man went to a lady and confessed to her he had lusted in his heart for her. This was sheer stupidity. That should have been confessed to God alone and been kept private. There are many sins of the heart or sins privately done which, if no one else is affected, should be kept private, especially anything involving sex. Personal sin, personal offenses, should be confessed personally.

If a Christian offends another person through losing his temper, or is unkind in word or deed, he should go to that one and apologize. This surely is what Matthew 5:22-24 is teaching. Many never will get a clear conscience until they have personally apologized.

One step further: public sin needs to be confessed publicly. If a brother has hurt the testimony of Christ and the whole church so that the community and church knows about it, he should confess before the whole church his wrong and his sorrow and apologize for it. This open apology has started many a revival.

Accept Forgiveness

A Christian needs to accept forgiveness from God by faith. He says, "If we confess our sins, he is faithful and just to forgive us our sins, and to cleanse us from all unrighteousness" (1 John 1:9). God is *faithful* to His promise and *just* because Christ already suffered for it. One must not depend on feelings, but on faith that he is immediately forgiven of the penalty and cleansed of the pollution.

Many Christians feel they have to do penance for each wrong deed. They do not *feel* forgiven and believe God stays mad at them for a few days or weeks at least. Often they will live in a state of uneasiness or have guilt feelings even after confessing their sins.

Remember man's ways are not God's ways. We sometimes expect God to react as we react. A person may say, "Yes, I forgive," but it takes days or weeks to get over being offended and hurt. Husbands and wives carry hurt feelings for days and show it even after they have apologized and made up. God isn't like that. He forgives and goes back to perfectly normal relations the moment one confesses his sin. What joy there is to realize this.

Someone may ask, "But what if I repeat the same sin?" Imagine yourself coming to God and saying, "Dear Lord, I did it again. Can you forgive me again?" The Lord would reply, "You did what again? Don't you recall I said, 'I'll remember them against you no more'? They are buried in the deepest sea and removed as far as the east is from the west." He says, "I don't know what you are talking about; I don't remember your having done anything before. Yes, I forgive you." Hallelujah! What a truth! Don't tremble or hesitate to trust the grace of God; confess the sin. If we are to forgive "seventy times seven," He surely will never be outdone!

The Curse of Unconfessed Sin

What if a Christian doesn't confess his sin? Will he still be saved? God says he will be chastened by the Lord, but he will "not be condemned with the world" (1 Cor. 11:32). He will still be saved, for Christ took the condemnation for them who are in Christ Jesus (Rom. 8:1).

Unconfessed sin leads to three things. One is chastening, or spanking. This includes God's taking away the fruit of the Spirit—no more love, joy, peace. Then, there will be no praise for the Lord Jesus. No praise is in the Christian's life or on his lips for Christ. He just can't say, "Praise the Lord!" It would choke him to try. Also, there will be no power in his life. Samson is a good example of that. The Christian's witnessing and teaching will be powerless.

Another possible result of not judging oneself is being set on the shelf by God and no longer used by Him. Paul greatly feared this for himself, for he said, "But I keep under my body, and bring it into subjection: lest that by any means, when I have preached to others, I myself should be a castaway" (1 Cor. 9:27). The word "castaway," as any Greek scholar will tell you, means "to be disapproved." In the context Paul is talking about his service for Christ. It is pictured as a contestant in a race or a boxing match. If the rules are broken, he is disapproved or disqualified and out of the race. He can no longer win the prize. If Christians do not deal with their sin, they can be disqualified from the race toward "the prize of the high calling of God in Christ Jesus" (Phil. 3:14). There must be many Christians in this state, for they do nothing for God. Saved, yes, but not in the race toward the prize.

A final result of unconfessed sin is to be cut off, or death. "He, that being often reproved hardened his neck, shall suddenly be destroyed, and that without remedy" (Prov. 29:1). "There is a sin unto death" (1 John 5:16). The key to the sin unto death is Proverbs 15:10: "Correction is grievous unto him that forsaketh the way: and he that hateth reproof shall die." God's correction, His chastening, is grievous and not joyous (Heb. 12:11).

The Christian should be exercised thereby and see the chastening yield the peaceable fruit of righteousness. If he doesn't react correctly, he will come to resent it and become bitter until he hates the reproof, and God may have to kill him. Hebrews 12:9 summarizes this when it says, "Furthermore we have had fathers of our flesh which corrected us, and we gave them reverence: shall we not much rather be in subjection to the Father of spirits, and live?" The writer in effect says, "Our earthly parents spank us, and we don't get bitter or sass them back. Then how much more should we reverence God and live?"

You see, if one doesn't reverence God, and resents God's chastening, God won't stand for insolence from His children and they won't live: "He shall die." There are many Christians in heaven who ought not to be there yet. They sinned the sin unto death—hated God's chastening until God killed them. What a warning this should be to judge ourselves and confess sin immediately.

One last word of warning. Don't spend too much time in introspection. To do this can bring terrible depression. God is faithful, and if one prays sincerely, "Search me, O God" (Ps. 139:23), he can be sure the Holy Spirit will do so. If there is sin, God will most certainly bring it to your mind. Don't let people like Job's friends accuse you and keep you in turmoil. God will show you if there is sin. If you are not convicted of sin after reading the Word and asking God to search you, trust Him that everything is all right. If you are facing darkness and trials, trust Him that they are testings and thank Him for them. "In every thing give thanks" (1 Thess. 5:18). "Count it all joy when ye fall into divers [testings]" (James 1:2). "Think it not strange concerning the fiery trial which is to try you . . . but rejoice, inasmuch as ye are partakers of Christ's suffering; that, when his glory shall be revealed, ye may be glad also with exceeding joy" (1 Pet. 4:12,13).

LEARNING TO WALK TAKES TIME

You have to walk by faith in the Spirit. You cannot walk by feelings. How long does it take for a baby to learn to walk? That's right, about one year. Remember this, *it takes about a year to learn to walk in the Spirit!* Did you get that? My daughter once said this was the greatest statement she ever heard me make. It helped her more than anything else had.

Remember that when your child took his first step he hadn't learned to walk yet. He stumbled over and over. What if, after stumbling, he had said, "I give up, it won't work"? He had to get back up and go again. A Christian will stumble many times before he learns to stay on his feet for any length of time. He must not give up. Even grown people who have been walking for years can stumble and must get up again. So Christians can walk with God for years and yet stumble somewhere along the way. Then, even if he's a preacher, he needs to confess sin and ask the Holy Spirit to take over again. Just make up your mind and say, "I'm going to walk in the Spirit."

Study Questions: Chapter 5

1. What is the spiritual roller coaster?
2. Discuss a Christian's dependence on the Holy Spirit in his walk in the Spirit.
3. What is involved in the expression "ye shall not fulfil the lusts of the flesh"?
4. How do you judge yourself?
5. Discuss confessing of sins.
6. Discuss forgiveness of a Christian's sins.
7. What are the results of a Christian not confessing his sins?

6
How on Earth Is the Spirit Quenched?

"Quench not the Spirit" (1 Thess. 5:19) is found only once in Scripture. Very little is written about it. The admonition is violated constantly, yet churches and Christians wonder why their lives are so empty and dry.

To "quench" means "squelch, stifle, or to put a stop to an urge." In modern terminology one could say, "Don't give the Holy Spirit the brush-off; don't snub the Holy Spirit." To "quench your thirst" is a common expression. What happens when you quench your thirst? You put a stop to the urge. This is precisely what one does when he quenches the Spirit. He puts a stop to an urge the Holy Spirit plants within him.

THE SPIRIT'S WORK BEFORE SALVATION

Christians are well aware of the work of the Holy Spirit within the unsaved. Before anyone can come to Christ, the Holy Spirit must "draw" him. Jesus said, "No man can come to me, except the Father which hath sent me draw him" (John 6:44). Though this is not elaborated upon, it is commonly held that the Father does the prompting of the Holy Spirit within a person.

Every Christian went through this before he was saved. Though he may not have been aware of it, the Holy Spirit worked on him over a period of time. Through trouble or tragedies God created the need and the desire in his heart to be saved. Through circumstances and invitations he went to church or was witnessed to by a Christian. God used this and began to draw him to Christ. Sometimes God does it by creating a hunger or thirst in one's heart. The person becomes tired of his life of sin and hungers for forgiveness. There comes a thirst to know God. All this is effected in one's heart by the Holy Spirit. It is part of His work today.

THE SPIRIT'S WORK AFTER SALVATION

There is also a definite work of the Holy Spirit in the heart of the believer, drawing and directing him into the will of God day by day. The key verse concerning this is Philippians 2:13, "For it is God which worketh in you both to will and to do of his good pleasure." What an instructive verse. It is God who works. In the Godhead the Person primarily operative today is the Holy Spirit. So it is God the Holy Spirit who works *in* you. God begins from within. God not only looks on the heart, but He begins His work there. Yes, He works on the outside through circumstances and other means, but too often Christians are not aware of that "still small voice" within.

Both are frequently overlooked. Yes, Christians quickly admit and say I can do nothing without the Lord, but what a difference to become conscious that I can *desire* to do nothing without the Lord. The Holy Spirit works within one to will, to desire, to do God's good pleasure or His will. You have no desire for God or good apart from the prompting, wooing, or working of the Holy Spirit.

Do you know what this means? It means every desire to read the Word of God comes from God. An urge to pray is from God. That burden for souls is from the Lord. The impulse to give out a tract or to witness to an individual must be from the Holy Spirit if one is walking in the Spirit. Multiply this into every avenue of life, and it has fantastic implications. God says emphatically, "Don't quench the Spirit." Respond! During the great Welsh revival Evan Roberts would stand before the people as he saw the evidence of the Holy Spirit working and plead with them, "Obey the Spirit!" That's it. Just obey and respond to the moving of the Holy Spirit. Don't give Him the brush-off. It is an offense to do so. It is sin.

The Heart of David

David was a man after God's own heart; one reason was that he did not quench the Spirit. There is a beautiful example of this in 2 Samuel 6. David was then king of the people of God. The ark of God, where God said He would dwell with His people, was in the hands of the enemy, the Philistines. David knew that the ark represented the presence of God. He knew that if he was going to rule the people of God well he needed God's presence and power. With this in mind, verse 2 tells us David went out to bring to Jerusalem "the ark of God, whose name is called by the name of the Lord of hosts that dwelleth between the cherubims."

In doing this David ignored the Word of God and tried to do a good thing in the wrong way! In Numbers 4 God gave instructions for moving the ark. It was to be carried by staves, which had been made for it, inserted through the rings on the side. Also the sons of Kohath were to be the ones to carry it. Most important, God said, "They shall not touch any holy thing, lest they die" (Num. 4:15). David ignored Scripture, and had the ark put on a new cart as the Philistines had done in 2 Samuel 6. Because of the first disobedience, the oxen shook the ark, and Uzzah put his hand on it to steady it. As God said He would do, God killed Uzzah (v. 7).

This scared David so severely that he cut short his project and left the ark with Obed-edom the Gittite (v. 10). God blessed Obed-edom immensely. Everything he touched turned to gold, as it were. The report came to David of how God was blessing Obed-edom "because of the ark of God." Well, that's all it took. David could stand it no longer, so he went after the ark again. He wanted God's blessing (v. 12). He got the ark and brought it into Jerusalem with great pomp and joy. As they entered the city, God tells us, "David danced before the Lord with all his might; and David was girded with a linen [girdle]. So David and all Israel brought up the ark of the Lord with shouting, and with sound of the trumpet" (2 Sam. 6:14,15).

Why Did David Dance?

Many have made reference to the dancing of David. Much has been said, but there is an aspect that is often missed. Why was David dancing? It was a common custom in those days that at the head of any parade or procession someone, usually a slave, would get out in front of the procession and dance up and down, much as a court jester would do, in honor of the one for whom the procession was made. This day King David's heart was so full that he himself took the lowly place of a slave and just danced up and down in honor of the Lord God of heaven. His own heart was so full, so full of joy, he wanted to do this honor himself. He did not quench the Spirit. He responded to his inner desire. He did not inhibit his emotions. They came with shouting. He did not consider or worry about what others would think of the king humbling himself so or of acting so undignified. He just did it "before the Lord."

Well, as it would happen, one nearest to him, his own wife, saw him through her window and "she despised him in her heart" (v. 16). She mocked him (v. 20). She probably curled her lips as she said, "How glorious was the king of Israel today, who uncovered himself today in the eyes of the handmaids of his servants, as one of the vain [or worthless] fellows shamelessly uncovereth himself!" (v. 20). And he said in a sense, "You don't understand. It was before the Lord that I danced. I wasn't doing it for show or shame. I just had to do it, and I'll do it again." Because Michal judged David wrongly and criticized him for what he did, God shut up her womb and she had no children "unto the day of her death" (v. 23). This was the worst thing that could have happened to a Jewish woman.

LIBERATING THE SPIRIT TODAY

Today many thirst for the presence and power of God. There seems to be a deep hunger among God's people. Many are tired of humdrum Christianity. Dry-eyed, dead, cold, calculating Christianity is out. People want to see the joy of the Lord. They want to see demonstrations of the power of God in transformed lives. So what do they do? They seek the Lord also, as it should be. God says, "Seek ye the Lord." Too often they do a good thing in a wrong way, as David did. They ignore the Word of God. There is a strong tendency today to ignore doctrine and scriptural teaching. Much is judged simply on the basis of experience and not on Scripture. For this reason there is a danger of getting detoured or defeated and having to face the judgment of God as Uzzah did. Some wonderful works of God and even Christian schools have gone the way of all flesh because they have tried to do God's work in unscriptural ways. Many Christians have been shipwrecked because they were misled. They then become afraid and give up as David did.

Finally, when a truly born-again Christian can stand it no longer, he will not be denied. When he once begins to find the secret of being Spirit-filled, he too will dance and shout for joy. Maybe not literally, but a new measure of joy will characterize his life. He will have an urge to come out with an "Amen!" or "Praise the Lord!" His heart may be so full he will want to weep. He may not have clapped to music before, but seeing others do it, he may want to try. God says, "Go ahead; don't quench the Spirit." This, in everyday living, is what it means.

God wants the Christian to walk in such obedience to the Holy Spirit that he responds to the slightest moving of the Spirit in his heart. God says, "Seek ye the Lord while he may be found, call ye upon him while he is near" (Isa. 55:6). Two things stand out in this verse: "while he may be found" and "while he is near." You see, God takes the initiative. He always does. Man is to respond to the moving of the Spirit. Apart from the Holy Spirit, Scripture declares, "There is none that seeketh after God" (Rom. 3:11). Not *some* seek after God, but *none* seek after God, unless He first works within them. At the slightest urge then (when He is near), a Christian should respond to the Spirit.

When the Lord Jesus was risen and met the two disciples on the Emmaus road, an interesting thing happened. They did not recognize the Lord Jesus. Their hearts "burned within them." Christ then "made as though he would have gone further" (Luke 24:28). They responded and "constrained him, saying, Abide with us," and He did. What a time they must have had. Whatever it means and however it is experienced, many Christians have had their hearts burn with a hunger and desire for God and His will. Some cry out to God and constrain Him to let them know all He wants them to know. Others simply quench the Spirit and never seem to catch on or see God doing great and mighty things.

Moses saw a bush burning, but it was not consumed (Exod. 3:2). Instead of ignoring it and going on his merry little way, he turned aside to see what was going on. He was never the same. God called him and said, "Draw not nigh [here]: put off thy shoes from off thy feet, for the place whereon thou standest is holy ground" (3:5). In mysterious ways God has tried to get the attention of many of His saints, but they "quench the Spirit." One evening D. L. Moody, the great evangelist, was noticed missing from the room where a number of people were having a good time of fellowship. When he showed up late, someone asked where he had been. He said that a burden to pray had come over him, and he had slipped away to get alone and pray. No wonder he saw so many of the wonders of God.

This most famous story of John Knox bears repeating. John Knox disappeared from a party one night. He was finally found in the garden on his knees crying out to God, "O God, give me Scotland or I die!" No wonder "Bloody Mary" said she "feared the prayers of John Knox more than all the armies of my enemies." Little wonder he was so mightily used of God in Scotland and all over Europe during the Reformation.

The Christian is to walk by faith and, in a sense, by feeling—that feeling being a sensitivity to the slightest moving of the Holy Spirit in his heart. Some Christians know nothing about such an experience. Such an idea may seem strange and foreign to their thinking. To a great company, though, this is very real. Such inclinations in the heart must be kept in line by the bounds of Scripture. God never leads contrary to His Word, no matter what visions or voices some claim to encounter.

Consider this: Every new idea, thought, hunch, brainstorm,

or desire you may have concerning spiritual things comes from God. He may be trying to attract your attention by a burning bush. He may be wanting to use you to witness to someone in unbelievable ways as He did Paul. Paul was not disobedient to the heavenly vision (Acts 26:19). Yours may not be a vision in the sky or the night, but remain obedient. Don't quench the Spirit. The average Christian knows little of that still, small voice within.

A little boy became afraid sleeping in a dark room all by himself. He went into his parents' room and asked to sleep with them. His father said, "Son, don't be afraid. You won't be alone; God is in there with you." He went back to his bedroom, peered through the door into the darkness, and said, "Dear God, if You're in there, don't You move, cause if You do You'll scare me to death." It almost appears that churches and Christians are saying to God today, "Don't You move in our church or in our hearts, for if You do, You will scare us to death!"

What has taken place during great revivals is upsetting to ultratraditionalists and conformists. What a joy it is to be liberated by the Holy Spirit and to let Him move and direct in marvelous ways as He so often did in the Book of Acts. Please, don't quench the Spirit the next time He moves in your heart. Respond and know the thrill of God at work in your life!

Study Questions: Chapter 6

1. What does the word quench mean?
2. How does one have a desire to do anything for God?
3. How did David do a right thing in a wrong way?
4. Why did David dance before the Lord?
5. What is the parallel to David's dancing in the Christian life today?
6. How do Christians quench the Holy Spirit?

7
What on Earth Grieves the Spirit?

"And grieve not the holy Spirit of God, whereby ye are sealed unto the day of redemption" (Eph. 4:30). If God says one should not grieve the Holy Spirit, then a Christian needs to understand what it means to grieve the Holy Spirit, what it is that grieves the Holy Spirit, and what the results are of grieving the Holy Spirit.

The word "grieve" in the Greek means what the English word is normally understood to mean. It means to cause sorrow, sadness, pain, or woe. When a person is grieved, it means he has been hurt, has been wronged. Someone has done something that brings sorrow and sadness. The Holy Spirit has emotions. He too can be hurt, for He is a sensitive Person in the right way.

What is it that grieves the Holy Spirit? Sin grieves the Holy Spirit. There is a difference, though, between how one grieves the Holy Spirit and how He is quenched. To simplify it, sins of commission grieve the Holy Spirit, and sins of omission quench the Spirit. One grieves the Spirit by doing what He tells him not to do, and one quenches the Spirit when he does not respond to what the Holy Spirit urged him to do. Grieving is a disobedience to His Word; quenching is a disobedience to His wooing.

Any sin, all sin, every sin, grieves the Holy Spirit. Obviously, murder, adultery, drunkenness, and similar sins grieve the Spirit. There would not be much dispute among Christians about those sins. What needs to be recognized as sins that grieve the Holy Spirit are some other things that Scripture seems to identify so they won't be missed.

Paul prayed for the Ephesians that they might know "what is the exceeding greatness of his power to us-ward who believe, according to the working of his mighty power, which he wrought in Christ, when he raised him from the dead"

(Eph. 1:19,20). Every Bible-believing, born-again pastor longs for that power in his ministry. Every soul-winning saint hungers for such power in witnessing. God knows the church needs it desperately today.

Many who once knew such power in their lives and ministries now feel helpless, as the world seems to be falling faster and faster into the power of sin and Satan. What's wrong? Too often we have grieved the Holy Spirit by sins that we somehow no longer call sins. They are what are often called "secret sins." These sins are like a short that drains all the power from a battery.

In meetings across North America I have been dumbfounded at what pastors and Christian workers have admitted or have been caught doing. One pastor who once knew the power of God in his ministry admitted being hooked on pornographic magazines. He is out of the ministry today. Another pastor had bitterness in his heart toward a deacon who had wronged him. His church finally split because he never did forgive, and the bitterness spread among the members. A friend of mine, a pastor in a large church, let his affections get turned toward a woman other than his wife. The blessing of God departed. He would not repent after being counseled at length. He, too, is out of the ministry.

These sins were hidden for a long time. The blessing and power of God were gone, and many people wondered why. The Holy Spirit was grieved. God just doesn't put up with believers grieving the Holy Spirit. Search your heart.

SINS THAT GRIEVE THE SPIRIT

Let's examine some of the often-overlooked sins that grieve the Holy Spirit. Look at the context in Ephesians 4 to see what grieves the Spirit. Verse 25 tells the Christian to put away lying and "speak the truth with his neighbor: for we are members one of another." Lying would seem to be quite evident as a sin, but the pressures of the world have broken down far too many fine Christians. Take the matter of lying on exams in school. You are under great pressure when "everyone else is doing it" to cheat just a little "to get by."

No, it grieves the Spirit for one to lie and claim some paper as his own or get the answers on a test from a classmate.

It is horrifying to hear of Christians claiming amounts given to God's work on income tax returns that are outright lies. Do you remember in Acts 5 how Ananias and Sapphira claimed to have given more than they actually had given? God killed them. In fact God said they lied to the Holy Spirit in so doing (Acts 5:3).

People make all kinds of promises and commitments about attending church, tithing, Bible reading, and then forget all about it. This is lying. It is better not to make a promise than to make it and not keep it (see Eccles. 5:4,5). God keeps His Word and expects man to do the same.

Another thing that grieves the Holy Spirit is unconfessed anger and wrath. "Don't let the sun go down on your wrath," God tells the Christian in Ephesians 4:26. This means it should be confessed and fellowship restored with the one wronged before the day is over. Sometimes when you have a decision to make, it is good to sleep on it for a while, but this is not the way to deal with wrath. Wrath seething inside will turn to bitterness unless it is dealt with. One must not wait a day to get things straightened out.

Nowhere is this needed more than in the home. Husbands and wives who have a quarrel must get it straightened out before going to bed. A wife is usually a far more sensitive person. If there has been a "little" spat, the husband may forget all about it, but the hurt in a wife lingers on. Later in bed when the husband wants to get romantic, his wife still may have the hurt and cannot respond. He then gets angry again and it goes from worse to worse. Often the truth never comes out. He never knows that it is his own fault his wife is cold and unresponsive. It may sound like a little thing, but husbands could warm up their wives in a minute with a genuinely warm apology. Apologizing is a lost practice today. The dividends are great, though. It could be the secret to transforming your life into glorious victory and continuous joy. Don't stay grieved. Get it off your chest; confess it.

Then God says, "Neither give place to the devil" (Eph.

4:27). A Christian is told, "Resist the devil, and he will flee from you" (James 4:7). When someone gives in to the devil, that person is to blame, for he has not claimed "the way to escape" by resisting Satan. Why is a Christian to blame? Because "greater is he that is in you, than he that is in the world" (1 John 4:4). "God has not given us the spirit of fear; but of power, and of love, and of a sound mind" (2 Tim. 1:7). Claim it! "This is the victory that overcometh the world, even our faith" (1 John 5:4).

Stealing grieves the Spirit; but God admonishes further to say of a man, "Let him labor, working with his hands the thing which is good, that he may have to give to him that needeth" (Eph. 4:28).

It is not enough just to stop stealing, but the Christian should start giving. He is to work, not so that he can have money to spend, but to give! That is what it says in the Word of God. How many live with this attitude? Do you? Why not try it and see how God blesses when you are not grieving the Spirit by working selfishly.

Next comes the admonition, "Let no corrupt communication proceed out of your mouth, but that which is good to the use of edifying, that it may minister grace unto the hearers" (Eph. 4:29). The word "corrupt" comes from a root word meaning "to rot off." It has the idea of destroying. What a Christian says should not destroy but edify, "build up," others.

Profanity grieves the Holy Spirit, but so does gossip and griping. These are corrupt communications as well. No doubt about it—this is the cause of many not seeing the mighty power of God working in their behalf. Nothing should come from a believer that would destroy another's character or testimony, but only that which edifies.

One of the most devastating sins that grieves the Holy Spirit is bitterness (Eph. 4:31). Again, it is not what happens to you but your reaction to it that really matters. Everyone has been hurt. Each of us could tell tales of being lied about or cheated. No one has escaped the crushing blow of being let down or betrayed by a trusted friend or even a loved one. What matters is what we do about it.

It is a sin to let it simmer inside until the heart is filled with bitterness. In the flesh one cannot forgive and forget, but by allowing the Holy Spirit to be in control, one can forgive and forget. The tragedy is that the one who is bitter is the one who suffers the most, not the one against whom the bitterness is held. Christians must not allow "any root of bitterness" to spring up "and thereby many be defiled" (Heb. 12:15).

Wrath is named next. This refers to outbursts of passion from inward indignation. Too often people "fly off the handle" and think nothing about it. Actually at that moment the Holy Spirit is grieved. It is not a Christlike reaction. The Holy Spirit then ceases to work through that one and works on him. Not confessing the sin causes him to be out of fellowship. Believers "blow up" all the time and go about their business as though it didn't make one bit of difference. The truth is, the power of God is shut off, even though the Christian does not realize it. The wise one will confess it immediately as sin and take appropriate action of apology if that is called for.

Anger suggests a more settled condition of mind with a view of taking revenge. When you think it through, it seems untenable that a born-again Christian could think of being angry to the point of revenge; but walking in the flesh, a believer is capable of doing this. This is the natural "work of the flesh."

Recently a deacon became angry with a preacher friend of mine. What this deacon did seemed impossible as he sought revenge, even though the pastor did all he could to rectify the situation. Remember, "Vengeance belongeth unto me, I will recompense, saith the Lord. And again, The Lord shall judge his people" (Heb. 10:30). What a relief to get rid of anger and let God save you from grieving the Spirit and being chastened of the Lord.

Clamor is an outcry like the tumult of a controversy. "The servant of the Lord must not strive" (2 Tim. 2:24). Arguing just cannot be condoned. Most marriages would be much happier if this sin were admitted to be grieving the Holy

Spirit and confessed as sin. The relationships of parents with their children would be much sweeter if parents, who should be more mature, would take the initiative to confess and forsake this sin.

Evil-speaking is the Greek word "blaspheme." It is often translated "railing." This could refer to sacreligious remarks or jokes. Humor is fine and often much needed, but never does one have to make jokes about religious things. Also, this refers to evil-speaking about some person when angry at him. The context seems to indicate this. Most of us wish we could have taken back some things said to a friend or loved one in a moment of anger. "The tongue is a fire, a world of iniquity; it is set on fire of hell" (James 3:6).

Malice means bad or evil. It probably has to do with evil actions as opposed to evil-speaking, such as getting even. This grieves the Holy Spirit. It is to be put away. It characterizes the world, not the child of God.

In another vein God indicates some positive actions that must be true of the child of God or he is grieving the Spirit. He says, "And be ye kind one to another" (Eph. 4:32). The world could use even a small dose of old-fashioned kindness to sweeten the atmosphere. The little girl who prayed for God to "make everybody a Christian and make Christians kind" must have sensed the need. Even God's children can be cruel. You would think we would all go out of our way to be kind. That wonderful, satisfying feeling of doing something kind for someone else with the right motive is priceless. This is living. This joy is the fuel for living life to the fullest. How long since you have tried it?

Christians are exhorted to be tenderhearted (see Eph. 4:32). Most married women today are starved to death for a little tender loving care from their husbands. Too many men have their wives for little more than a maid and a mistress. Husbands need to "try a little tenderness."

Forgive "one another, even as God for Christ's sake hath forgiven you" (Eph. 4:32). Cancer can kill, but it is trivial compared to the heartache caused by a lack of forgiveness. How a person can stand bearing the burdens of bitterness and resentment is a mystery no one can explain. I've done things others don't know about that God has forgiven me for. How then can I hold something against someone else? You too, no doubt, have sins for which you have been forgiven. How then can you be unforgiving of someone else?

THE RESULTS OF GRIEVING THE SPIRIT

What happens when you grieve the Holy Spirit? He ceases to work through you and begins working on you. The fruit of the Spirit is no longer produced. Love, joy, and peace shrivel up. Everything begins to go sour. The trouble then is not in your job, your loved one, your teacher in school. It is the one you see in the mirror each day who has stopped the flow of joy. When David sinned and made his confession, he cried out, "Restore unto me the joy of thy salvation" (Ps. 51:12). You "turn on the spout where the joy comes out" by confessing and forsaking not only the obviously immoral sins, but the "little foxes that spoil the vines" (Song of Sol. 2:15).

When you are grieved at anything but sin, you can be sure the Holy Spirit is grieved. Stop and confess. The longer one rationalizes, the more one loses. The excuses one makes for his mistakes are often worse than the mistake. How wonderful to have a clear conscience by confessing that one has sinned and grieved the Holy Spirit.

Study Questions: Chapter 7

1. What is the distinction between grieving and quenching the Spirit?
2. What are some of the "secret sins" of Christians that grieve the Holy Spirit?
3. Why is bitterness referred to as "the most devastating sin"?
4. Explain the difference between wrath and anger.
5. What are some things a Christian must do so he does not grieve the Holy Spirit?
6. What are the consequences of grieving the Spirit?

8
How on Earth Can I Be Saved?

There was a pistol on the table. He was ready to commit suicide. His wife had left him. For three weeks he had been drunk and was totally depressed. I had just told him the greatest story I ever heard about the most wonderful person I ever met: the gospel of the Lord Jesus Christ. I began to pray. After about three sentences Frank blurted out, "Preacher, I'm saved; preacher, something just happened to me!" What a way to have a prayer meeting broken up! He had been a nervous wreck, twitching every few seconds. Under the influence of alcohol his speech had been slurred. When he blurted out, "I'm saved," I looked up. He was as sober as I! No longer did he twitch; his speech was as clear and articulate as mine. What had happened? He was saved, that's what! In a moment he was "born again," just as the Bible says that one must be to "enter the kingdom of God." Since then his wife has returned, they attend church, and he hasn't touched liquor.

A woman had visited a psychiatrist regularly for years and spent a fortune on doctors, but she was an emotional and almost a physical wreck. Her psychiatrist had dismissed her, saying, "I can't do you any good." She tried to see a woman psychiatrist, but this psychiatrist did not have any open time. She met some Christians, saw their joy, heard the gospel, and accepted Christ as her Savior. Her life was transformed. When the woman psychiatrist called her a week later telling her she could now take her, the woman said, "I don't need you now. I have found what I've needed and am a changed person." What had happened to her? She had been saved, born again.

WHAT MUST I DO TO BE SAVED?

Seeing just such a difference in others, a jailor wisely

asked, "What must I do to be saved?" (Acts 16:30). The term *saved* is a sound biblical term and should be in every Christian's vocabulary. There are dozens of Scriptures with the words *save* or *saved,* referring to an act of God by which one becomes a changed person on the inside, resulting in a change in one's outward behavior. What is a Christian? He is a *saved* person! "How does one become saved?" "What must I do to be saved?" Most people would rather risk catastrophe than ask directions!

God declares, "The gospel of Christ . . . is the power of God unto salvation to every one that believeth" (Rom. 1:16). What is the gospel? Many are familiar with the "Romans Road" as a way to present the gospel. It starts with Romans 3:23, "For all have sinned, and come short of the glory of God." We are all in the same boat, aren't we? We have all sinned. God declares, "There is none righteous, no, not one" (Rom. 3:10). No truly honest person would dare declare, "I have never done wrong; I have never sinned." The Scripture declares in 1 John 1:8, "If we say that we have no sin, we deceive ourselves, and the truth is not in us." Everyone has to admit to human weakness and failure, whether it be lying to parents as a child, cheating in school, anger, hate, evil thoughts, or immorality. Man has broken the laws of God and must face the penalty.

The penalty, God states, is death, for "the wages of sin is death" (Rom. 6:23). Death is separation. Physical death is the separation of one's life from his physical body. This is the first death. Spiritual death is separation of one's life from God. This is the second death (see Rev. 21:8). To some this seems an awful penalty, but that is because they have a wrong view of God. God is a holy God and cannot permit sin to go unpunished. Sin cannot be permitted in the presence of God. His character demands that sin be punished and the sinner be banished from His presence. Therefore, one who dies in his sin must be banished from God's presence (John 8:24).

But there is good news, for "God commendeth his love toward us, in that, while we were yet sinners, Christ died for us" (Rom. 5:8). Why did Christ die two thousand years ago?

Because death is the wages of sin and He paid for our sins in full! It wasn't an easy, cheap payment: "For Christ also hath once suffered for sins, the just for the unjust, that he might bring us to God" (1 Pet. 3:18).

Christ did not just die physically, though that death was very real; He also died spiritually. He was separated from God when He cried, "My God, my God, why hast thou forsaken me?" (Mark 15:34). The answer is simple: Then and there He suffered for sins and experienced the anguish of separation from God. He indeed suffered physically, but the inward suffering was the suffering for sins.

Something wonderful and eternal happened at that time, for the Bible declares that Christ "is the propitiation for our sins" (1 John 2:2). The word "propitiation" means "satisfaction." Christ satisfied the righteous demands of a holy God and paid the just payment for the sins of the world.

An illustration of that would be to suppose that I owed you ten thousand dollars and didn't have a dime. Then suppose a friend said, "Sumner, I love you, let me pay that debt for you. You can't pay him, and I know you can't pay me either. I want to give you the money." If my friend counted out ten thousand dollars in cash and gave you the money, I wouldn't owe you a dime even though I didn't pay it myself. You wouldn't say, "Give me one more nickel." You would be *satisfied*. You would be paid in full. The Lord Jesus cried, "It is finished" (John 19:30). He paid the debt in full. God is propitiated. He is satisfied. Three days later Christ rose from the dead and is alive forevermore. That is the gospel. That is the Good News men need to heed.

What is left, then, to being saved? "If thou shalt confess with thy mouth the Lord Jesus, and shalt believe in thine heart that God hath raised him from the dead, thou shalt be saved" (Rom. 10:9). As Paul said to the Philippian jailor, "Believe on the Lord Jesus Christ, and thou shalt be saved" (Acts 16:31). It is simple to believe in and put your trust in what the Lord Jesus did on the cross for you. This is not blind faith. Most people have faith, but their faith is in *their* deeds instead of in *Christ's deed* on the cross. God never

91

promised to save anyone for doing anything. He did promise to save those who "believe on the Lord Jesus Christ." The emphatic statement of Scripture is, "Not by works of righteousness which we have done, but according to his mercy he saved us" (Titus 3:5).

PENALTY AND POLLUTION

There is another aspect to what Christ did to save us that is presented in Figure 9.

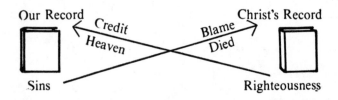

Figure 9.

Our "record" is a long list of sins. We are all in the same boat; we have all sinned. The Bible says, "All we like sheep have gone astray; we have turned every one to his own way" (Isa. 53:6).

Two things result from sin: a penalty and a pollution. The penalty of death is common knowledge. The awareness of the pollution of sin is less common. Suppose you had a ten-gallon jug of pure, clean, fresh water and someone poured one drop of filth into that water. You wouldn't drink that water. It would be polluted. That one drop would contaminate the whole jug of water. It would be unclean, unfit to drink. So it is with sin. Just one sin is all it takes to pollute man spiritually so that he is unclean, unfit for heaven. Thanks be to God, there is a provision for both the penalty and the pollution. The death of Christ takes care of the penalty, and the blood of Christ takes care of the pollution, for "the blood of Jesus Christ his Son cleanseth us from all sin" (1 John 1:7).

Look for a moment at the diagram under "Christ's Record" (in Figure 9), and you will see the word "righteousness." He had no pollution, for "in him was no sin." Judas said, "I have betrayed the innocent blood" (Matt. 27:4). Then He was under no penalty, for He "knew no sin" (2 Cor. 5:21). Pilate himself said, "I find no fault in him" (John 19:6). Indeed, no one ever has or could ever find any fault in Him. He was perfect. He was righteous. Yes, He truthfully said, "I do always those things that please [the Father]" (John 8:29).

The whole Bible is summed up by Figure 9. Two thousand years ago God took all the sins under our name and put them on Christ's record. He took the blame for all we did and suffered and died as though He actually had done what we did. There is no other explanation for the death of Christ except that God "laid on him the iniquity of us all" (Isa. 53:6). Not only did He pay the penalty, but He shed His blood to take care of the pollution, for the blood of Jesus Christ, God's Son, cleanses us from all sin (see 1 John 1:7). What an astounding revelation that is! God speaks of "the washing of regeneration" (Titus 3:5). "Unto him that loved us, and washed us from our sins in his own blood" (Rev. 1:5).

What a great relief to know the guilt and stain of sin can be completely removed! No wonder it is called "so great salvation" (Heb. 2:3).

With all this, there still remains the common question of being "good enough" to go to heaven. Bless God, He has made provision for this as well. Figure 9 shows that now God wants to take Christ's righteousness and put that on our account. We get credit for what Christ did; we go to heaven as though we ourselves had done what He did. Scripture says, "The righteousness of God which is . . . unto all and upon all them that believe" (Rom. 3:22). One verse contains both transfers shown in Figure 9: God "made him to be sin for us, who knew no sin; that we might be made the righteousness of God in him" (2 Cor. 5:21).

This, too, can be understood by a simple illustration. Suppose someone went to the bank and deposited one million dollars in the bank in your name. They just gave you one million dollars. Even though you didn't earn it or deserve it, you would be a millionaire.

So it is with all who believe on the Lord Jesus Christ as their Savior. The righteousness of Christ is deposited to their account, and they have all the righteousness needed to get into heaven, "for Christ is the end of the law for righteousness to every one that believeth" (Rom. 10:4). His righteousness allows them to enter heaven, not their own righteousness. "All our righteousnesses are as filthy rags" (Isa. 64:6), and they could never make a person acceptable to God.

The Jews of Paul's day were "ignorant of God's righteousness, and going about to establish their own righteousness, [and had] not submitted themselves unto the righteousness of God" (Rom. 10:3). As so many today, they were trying to make themselves good enough for heaven, trying to "establish their own righteousness." Even as many today, the Jews were ignorant of the righteousness provided by God that alone could have made them acceptable, and thus they never applied for or submitted themselves to this righteousness.

What must I do to be saved? The transfer of man's sin to the Lord Jesus took place two thousand years ago.

When does the transfer of the righteousness of Christ occur? When a person by faith receives the Lord Jesus as Savior. It happens the moment one from his heart "believes on the Lord Jesus Christ." The question is not how much faith one has, but what that person's faith is in.

THE RIGHT KIND OF FAITH

Of those in the world who have some inclination to believe in God there are basically two groups: One group believes in what they are *doing* to get them to heaven. They expect God to let them in heaven because of things they have done or are doing. These are not atheists or agnostics; these are professing Christians—both laity and preachers—who are still ignorant of God's righteousness and are trying to establish their own righteousness. They believe salvation is the reward of good works. The terrifying end, Jesus said, is, "I never knew you: depart from me" (Matt. 7:23). You can't live right, nor die right, unless you believe right.

The second group believes that *what the Lord Jesus did* is the only way to heaven. They "believe on the Lord Jesus Christ" to be saved. These can sing with real understanding:

> Just as I am, without one plea
> But that Thy blood was shed for me,
> And that Thou bid'st me come to Thee,
> O Lamb of God, I come! I come!

> Just as I am, Thou wilt receive,
> Wilt welcome, pardon, cleanse, relieve;
> Because Thy promise I believe,
> O Lamb of God, I come! I come!

They expect to go to heaven, not for anything they have done, but only because the Lord Jesus suffered and died for them. These can speak of the finished work of Christ on the cross, meaning He left nothing for them to do to be saved but trust what He did to get them to heaven. They are truly "born of God" and have a genuinely changed life as a result of the new birth. No wonder Paul's simple answer to the profound question, "What must I do to be saved?" was, "Believe on the Lord Jesus Christ, and thou shalt be saved" (Acts 16:30,31).

HOW CAN I BE SURE I'M SAVED?

Suppose God were to say to you personally, "You have everlasting life; you are saved." Would you be sure, then, that you are saved? Of course you would. Well, the Bible is just as true as if God said it out loud to you personally. In effect, God is saying, "You really want to know who has everlasting life? Well, I'll tell you." He says, "He that believeth on the Son hath everlasting life" (John 3:36), not "he that believes in doing the best he can" or "he that believes in his baptism" or "in his church" or in anything else but the Son. He didn't say "might have" or "would someday have" or "would feel as if"; He said *has*, right now, everlasting life! Who said so? God did! Now, do you believe on the Son to get you to heaven? You say, "Yes, I do!" Then do you have "everlasting life"? If you can say, "Yes, I surely do, because God said so," that is saving *faith* that came by the Word of God (Rom. 10:17).

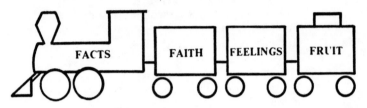

Figure 10.

The engine of the little train depicted in Figure 10 represents the *facts* of the Word of God. The facts are irrevocable. "Christ died for [our sins]" (Rom. 5:8). "If thou shalt confess with thy mouth . . . and shalt believe in thine heart that God has raised him from the dead, thou shalt be saved" (Rom. 10:9).

Faith is taking God at His Word. It is believing God in spite of feelings or anything else that Satan might bring to one's attention to make him doubt what God said to be true.

Feelings and fruit (the caboose) are not essential and should not be depended on or trusted for the assurance of salvation. It ought to be simply, "God said it, I believe it, and that settles it." Too often people want not only the facts but also the feeling before they will have the faith that they are saved. It doesn't work that way. People may have all kinds of emotional experiences and never be born again. This is why churches are so full of individuals who have never proved to be "a new creature: old things are passed away; behold, all things are become new" (2 Cor. 5:17).

Right now I don't have a feeling inside that says, "Now you are married." I know I'm married on the basis of a simple fact: One day I said, "Yes, I receive this woman as my wife." God says, "As many as received him [the Lord Jesus Christ], to them gave he power to become the sons of God, even to them that believe on his name" (John 1:12). God doesn't give some funny feeling that says, "Now you're saved." I know right now I'm saved because I believed on the Lord Jesus Christ as my Savior, and I received Him into my heart. He said, "I stand at the door, and knock: if any man hear my voice, and open the door, I will come in" (Rev. 3:20). Did you hear His voice? Did you invite Him in? Did He keep His Word?

If you haven't already done so, bow your head, invite Him in, and thank Him for saving you.

Study Questions: Chapter 8

1. What is the meaning of the word "propitiation"?
2. What are the two basic results of sin?
3. Explain the basis upon which God can righteously save us. (Use the diagram.)
4. Into what groups of people can the whole world be divided?
5. Explain the relationship between facts, faith, and feelings using the train analogy.

9
What on Earth Happened to Me?

Some people watch things happen, others make things happen, but sorrowfully, many never know what has happened at all. At the moment an individual is saved, many fantastic eternal things happen. There are five specific ministries of the Holy Spirit performed in the life of each believer. Regretfully, many Christians are never taught these great truths, which are fundamental. It is vitally important to know these truths and to build on them. Belief determines behavior. If our beliefs are unknown or uncertain or unfounded, it will have a profound effect upon our living. So we want to see what happened to you the moment you were saved.

BORN OF THE SPIRIT

First of all, you were "born again" or "born of the Spirit." In John 3:5–7, Jesus said, "Verily, verily, I say unto thee, Except a man be born of water and of the Spirit, he cannot enter into the kingdom of God. That which is born of the flesh is flesh; and that which is born of the Spirit is spirit. Marvel not that I said unto thee, Ye must be born again." This new birth brings you into a *relationship* with God; you become a "son of God."

Relationship is based on birth; fellowship is based on behavior. There is a vast difference. Many who overlook this vital fact have great turmoil, not being certain of their salvation. It is this act by which life comes. In the natural realm it is so, and just as certainly it is so in the spiritual realm. When one is born of earthly parents, he gets the same kind of life as his earthly parents: physical and temporal. When born of God, one gets God's kind of life: spiritual and eternal. This is why in John's Gospel alone God tells the believer over one hundred times that he has everlasting or eternal life. Just as an earthly child could not get unborn of his earthly parents, so one born of God can never get unborn of God. The relationship is permanent. Yes, a child may disobey his parents and be out of favor and fellowship with his parents, but still that one is by blood, by birth, a child of his father and mother. So one born of God may sin and lose favor and fellowship with his heavenly Father, but he will not lose the relationship. Christ is "in him," and he declared, "I will never leave thee" (Heb. 13:5).

Through this act of the Holy Spirit one gets his new nature; he is a partaker of the divine nature (2 Pet. 1:4). Everything produces after its kind (Gen. 1:24,25). Even so, one "born of God" has this "divine nature" in him that will constantly strive against the sin nature and long to obey God. "As newborn babes, desire the sincere milk of the word, that ye may grow thereby" (1 Pet. 2:2). When someone is born, that one is a baby and needs feeding to grow. So it is spiritually; Christians must feed on the Word of God. As a new babe needs frequent feedings, so do Christians. One meal on Sunday just won't do! It is a long, long process, but it all begins by birth.

SEALED BY THE SPIRIT

One of the most profound and most precious truths is the ministry of the Holy Spirit by which a believer is "sealed unto the day of redemption" (Eph. 4:30). This work of the Holy Spirit is spoken of in Ephesians 1:13 and also in 2 Corinthians 1:22.

A seal was a significant thing in Bible times. Most people today are aware of the fact that people had signet rings in those days. These rings were specially made, such as a branding iron is today. Each person had his own sign or design. When someone sent a letter or scroll he melted wax to seal the scroll, and he pressed his sign into the wax with his ring. This had several significant purposes.

First, it showed ownership. If this sign were placed on anything, it showed who owned it. The Holy Spirit Himself is the sign of ownership. The Holy Spirit in the believer is a sure sign he belongs to God, for "if any man have not the

Spirit of Christ, he is none of his" (Rom. 8:9). A Christian is owned and gladly claimed by God. A Christian has the glorious assurance that he belongs to God.

The seal also meant security. No one dared to open or break the seal until it was delivered to its destination. Of course, when something bore the king's seal, it was secure until it arrived at its destination. Being sealed by the King of Kings brings great security. God says the believer is sealed "unto the day of redemption." This is that final day when the body, too, shall be redeemed and delivered into the presence of the King. This sealing is once and final and lasts to the time of complete deliverance from all sin. The sealing is done by the Holy Spirit, and the Christian is "kept by the power of God" (1 Pet. 1:5). The security of the believer runs through Scripture from cover to cover.

Sealing signified a finished transaction. When the seal was affixed to a letter, it meant the whole matter was settled. The Lord Jesus Christ cried, "It is finished." His part was complete. The purchase price was paid for man's salvation. When man by faith affixes his okay on it and believes on the Lord Jesus as His Savior, too, the transaction of salvation and the new birth is sealed by the Holy Spirit; it is a finished transaction. What the Christian does, then, has a lot to do with his rewards in heaven and God's blessing upon him here and now, but his *salvation* is "sealed unto the day of redemption."

This sealing is done simultaneously with the receiving of the Holy Spirit, as 2 Corinthians 1:22 indicates. Of course, this occurs at the moment of salvation. It is not something that only super-spiritual Christians attain, for even the carnal Corinthians had been sealed by the Holy Spirit. No one is ever exhorted to seek it, for it comes automatically as does the new birth when one trusts Christ (see Eph. 1:13). It is never repeated, for one is "sealed unto the day of redemption." Since the Holy Spirit is to abide in the believer forever (see John 14:16,17), this truth gives great assurance and rejoicing to every believing heart who trusts the Word of God.

BAPTISM OF THE SPIRIT

The baptism of the Holy Spirit, the third ministry of the

Holy Spirit to the believer, has brought much controversy and confusion to many people. While it is not the intent of this book to deal with the total doctrine of the baptism of the Holy Spirit, but only to look at the baptism of the Holy Spirit relative to the Christian's spiritual life, a doctrinal foundation needs to be laid. Dr. John F. Walvoord in his book *The Holy Spirit* has an excellent summary of the doctrinal problem:

> The confusion prevailing in the treatment of this doctrine has its rise in many factors. The principal cause of disagreement is found in the common failure to apprehend the distinctive nature of the church. Many theologians regard the church as a universal group of saints of all ages, some extending even these boundaries to include in the conception of all who outwardly belong to it, even if not saved. If this concept of the nature of the church is held, the baptism of the Holy Spirit has no relation to it. As this ministry is not found in the Old Testament and is not included in any prophecies regarding the millennium, it is peculiarly the work of the Holy Spirit for the present age, beginning with Pentecost and ending at the resurrection of the righteous when the living church is translated. If, however, the church be defined as the saints of this age only, the work of the Holy Spirit in baptizing all true believers into the body of Christ takes on a new meaning. It becomes the distinguishing mark of the saints of the present age, the secret of the peculiar intimacy and relationship of Christians to the Lord Jesus Christ. It is, therefore, essential to a proper doctrine of the baptism of the Holy Spirit that it be recognized as the distinguishing characteristic of the church, the body of Christ.

Several things should be noted about the baptism of the Holy Spirit. It occurs at the moment of salvation, for "if any man be in Christ, he is a new creature: old things are passed away; behold, all things are become new" (2 Cor. 5:17). How does one get "in Christ"? He is "baptized into one body by the one and the same Spirit." This is the work of the Holy Spirit placing a believer "in Christ." Christ is the head; the believers are the body. From then on, God sees the believer "in Christ." This is a positional truth. He then stands before God in Christ, fully credited with all that Christ is. This is a profound truth and the ramifications are numerous. It is because of this that the Christian can say, "I am crucified with Christ" (Gal. 2:20). Also, the believer is "risen with Christ" (Col. 3:1). Being "in Christ," a person stands before God as righteous as the Son, for "the righteousness of God . . . is . . . unto all and upon all them that believe" (Rom. 3:22).

Every Christian has already been baptized by the Holy Spirit. It is a tragic mistake to exhort those already saved to seek to be baptized by the Holy Spirit. Paul said to the carnal Christians, "By one Spirit are [or were] we *all* baptized into one body." The Greek and the context indicate this to be a past action. It is not some super-spiritual experience that one has after he is saved. All Christians are baptized by the Spirit at the moment of salvation.

To be baptized with the Holy Spirit is entirely different than being filled with the Holy Spirit. God doesn't use words and terms loosely. No one would mind being baptized in a thousand gallons of water but would certainly object to any attempt to be filled with a thousand gallons of water. There is a vast difference between the two experiences. Some erroneously say the two terms of Scripture are the same, and often, in writing and in speaking, use the terms interchangeably. This is absolutely unacceptable hermeneutically. It shows a gross lack of spiritual discernment and a sloppy use of biblical terminology.

One of the greatest mysteries of all time is that the Greek word *baptizo* was not translated in the King James Version of the Bible or most other versions. Had it been, much confusion would have been avoided in several areas of doctrine. *Baptizo* means "to immerse, dip, or submerge." An entirely different word, *rhantizo,* means to "sprinkle." The significance here is that the believer is immersed or submerged into the body of Christ. He is placed spiritually into this union with all other believers in Christ.

Each believer's place is unique and individual. One is, as

it were, a hand, another a foot (1 Cor. 12:14ff.). Each Christian has a specific position and function. Just as in one's physical body no one would desire to get rid of any part of his body, so every believer is needed and important in the body of Christ (1 Cor. 12:21,22).

The wonderful truth of the baptism of the Spirit and all its results is so "that there should be no schism [division] in the body" (1 Cor. 12:25). It is revealing that the results of the teaching that the baptism of the Spirit should be sought by those already in Christ, and that it is accompanied by what is called "speaking in tongues," has brought division. Churches by the score have been split, families have been divided, and Christians across the country have been separated into different camps over this misuse of the doctrine.

The right understanding of the truth unites Christians. It gives a greater appreciation of one another. Each depends on the others more. Christians feel the need of other Christians, rather than feeling superior to others because of this doctrine. Beliefs that bring wrong behavior should be carefully examined. God isn't the author of confusion (1 Cor. 14:33). Every believer can rejoice that he already has been baptized into one body. He too is in Christ and has been blessed "with all spiritual blessings in heavenly places in Christ" (Eph. 1:3). He need not seek some false hope of a second blessing or some false doctrine of a baptism of the Spirit as a panacea. If he will "walk by faith," "in the Spirit," and be "filled with [controlled by] the Spirit," he will have all the fruit and the power of Pentecost he can absorb.

INDWELT BY THE SPIRIT

Jesus, speaking to His disciples, said that the Holy Spirit "dwelleth with you, and shall be in you" (John 14:17). The Holy Spirit has ministered in all ages, but He has taken up a permanent residence in the believer since the day of Pentecost.

In the Old Testament the Holy Spirit came upon individuals, but He did not dwell in them permanently. David could therefore pray, "Take not thy holy spirit from me" (Ps. 51:11). Of Samson it is said, "The Spirit of the Lord came mightily upon him" (Judg. 15:14). Then because of his sin, the Holy Spirit left him and he knew "not that the Lord was departed from him" (Judg. 16:20). Without the Holy Spirit working through him, Samson said, "I shall become weak, and be like any *other* man" (Judg. 16:17, italics mine).

Today the Holy Spirit dwells in every believer *forever*. What a great promise and provision! Once again it is said to the carnal Corinthians, "What? know ye not that your body is the temple of the Holy Ghost which is in you, which ye have of God, and ye are not your own?" (1 Cor. 6:19). The Holy Spirit does not come into just *some* believers or into super-spiritual believers but into *all* believers. Many may not be aware of Him today, but He is there nonetheless, even as He was with those Corinthians, "for if any man have not the Spirit of Christ, he is none of his" (Rom. 8:9). It is unscriptural to pray the prayer of David, "Take not thy holy spirit from me," for Jesus declared He would be in us "forever."

It needs repeating here that the church, the body of Christ, is a "habitation of God through the Spirit" (Eph. 2:22), and so it is that "Christ liveth in me" (Gal. 2:20) in the person of the Holy Spirit. Just as the Lord Jesus could say, "He that hath seen me hath seen the Father" (John 14:9), so we can say that he who has the Holy Spirit has Christ, and he who has the Son has the Holy Spirit. What security this truth brings when God says, "I will never leave thee" (Heb. 13:5), and the Holy Spirit is to "abide with you for ever" (John 14:16).

With the Holy Spirit living in the Christian, it becomes easy to understand the injunction, "Grieve not the holy Spirit" (Eph. 4:30). The Holy Spirit is in the Christian to lead him, teach him, fill him, and perform many other ministries expressed in Scripture. Thus, it behooves a Christian to "quench not the Spirit" (1 Thess. 5:19), but allow him to do all He came to do in and through the believer.

There is a difference between the Holy Spirit dwelling in us and the Holy Spirit filling us. No Christian is exhorted to be indwelt by the Holy Spirit; he already is. But every believer is exhorted to be filled or controlled by the Holy Spirit. Every Christian *possesses* the Holy Spirit, but the Holy Spirit doesn't *possess* every Christian. Just as people are spoken of as being possessed, usually meaning by an evil spirit, so Christians need to be possessed by the Holy Spirit who dwells in them.

ANOINTED BY THE SPIRIT

Another term that is sometimes taken to be the same as the initial act of indwelling of the Holy Spirit is the anointing of the Holy Spirit. This is spoken of as a past action in the believer's life in 2 Corinthians 1:21 and 1 John 2:20,27. The Lord Jesus is said to have been anointed "with the Holy Ghost and with power" (Acts 10:38).

While it may be true that the anointing is the initial act of indwelling or that it takes place then, at least there seems to be more significance to the anointing. First, in Luke 4:18 it is stated of the Lord Jesus, "The Spirit of the Lord is upon me, because he hath anointed me to preach the gospel to the poor." This seems to indicate equipping of the Lord for His ministry. This could compare to Acts 1:8 when God says, "Ye shall receive power . . ."

Every Christian is anointed and equipped with the power of the Holy Spirit for ministering with his gifts to the glory of the Lord. Everyone in the family of God is to be a part of the ministry of the Lord on earth. Each is assured of being anointed to this ministry.

In the Old Testament, kings and priests were anointed with oil as they were consecrated to their service. This anointing with oil is comparable to our anointing today. Jesus said, "Ye have not chosen me, but I have chosen you, and ordained you, that ye should go and bring forth fruit, and that your fruit should remain" (John 15:16).

Then in 1 John 2:20,27 this anointing is associated with spiritual discernment and teaching of the things of God. In the anointing of the Holy Spirit, God assures the believer that he can understand the things of God and be taught by the Holy Spirit Himself. Every Christian can't go to Bible school or seminary, but, thank God, he doesn't have to, for the Holy Spirit will show him wonderful things out of the Word.

As a boy I remember how the father of one of my best friends would sit on his porch and read a large family Bible by the hour. This man, named Mr. Oliver, had never gone to high school. At the time I wasn't a Christian, but it made a deep impression on me. Years later, after being saved and going to seminary, I went to see him. It was the first time I had seen him since I was saved. We visited for a couple of hours. I was overwhelmed by his knowledge of the Word of God. We had rich fellowship. As I left with tears in my eyes and glory in my soul, the truth of how the Holy Spirit can teach a childlike believer the things of God became real and has been a help to me for years.

Each of us had so much happen to us the moment we were saved. It is a tragedy that more don't realize it and take advantage of the Holy Spirit's work in our lives. Why not reflect right now on these things, thank God for them, then act on them and see your life become more fruitful and meaningful day by day.

Study Questions: Chapter 9

1. What five things happen simultaneously at the moment of salvation?
2. Explain the difference between relationships and fellowship.
3. For what length of time is a believer "sealed"?
4. What is the meaning of the Greek word *baptizo?*
5. Explain the difference between the presence of the Holy Spirit in the life of believers in the Old Testament as compared to His presence in believers today.

10
What on Earth Made Me Do It?

I don't want to sin. I don't want to hurt God. I don't want to put Christ to an open shame. "As the hart [deer] panteth [longs] after the water brooks, so panteth my soul after thee, O God. My soul thirsteth after God" (Ps. 42:1,2). How many times has this been the cry of your soul? Remember the times when you have thought your breast would burst, and you have sobbed in your soul after God? You cried out in your heart, "Here I am, Lord; take all of me." You meant every word of it, and then six weeks later you were doing things you couldn't believe were possible. You sinned in a way that seemed totally unreal. You cried out, "What made me do it? How on earth could I, after loving the Lord so much and yielding all I had to Him?"

It is simple; it is "sin that dwelleth in me" (Rom. 7:17). Not to understand this can lead to total disaster. To understand what "made you do it" can lead to being forewarned and forearmed, which lead to victory.

Paul had the same problem:

> For that which I do I allow not: for what I would, that do I not; but what I hate, that do I. If then I do that which I would not, I consent unto the law that it is good. Now then it is no more I that do it, but sin that dwelleth in me.
>
> For I know that in me (that is, in my flesh,) dwelleth no good thing: for to will is present with me; but how to perform that which is good I find not. For the good that I would I do not: but the evil which I would not, that I do. Now if I do that I would not, it is no more I that do it, but sin that dwelleth in me.
>
> I find then a law, that, when I would do good, evil is present with me. For I delight in the law of God after the inward man: But I see another law in my members, warring against the law of my mind, and bringing me into captivity

to the law of sin which is in my members. O wretched man that I am! who shall deliver me from the body of this death? I thank God through Jesus Christ our Lord. So then with the mind I myself serve the law of God; but with the flesh the law of sin (Rom. 7:15-25).

THE TUG OF WAR

This is the great dilemma every believer faces. Paul personifies the believer's two natures, the new nature wanting to do good and the sin nature wanting to do evil. Each is represented by an "I": "I" is part of the new man who longs and thirsts for God, and "I" is an urge to sin.

We speak of the law of gravity or the pull of gravity. This is exactly the way Paul describes the sin nature or flesh we all possess. He calls it a "law" in verses 21 and 25. It is specifically called the "law of sin" in verse 25. It is that pull to sin, that force or urge that keeps cropping up, even after the child of God has had a great dramatic experience with God and has yielded everything to Him.

In one song, "Love Divine," we sing, "Take away our bent to sinning." The old theologians talked much about the "propensity to sin" or the "bent to sinning." The truth is we all have it. In another song, a chorus, "Let the beauty of Jesus be seen in me," we sing, "All my nature refine." The truth is the old sin nature can never be refined. It is folly to think so and foolishness to pray for it. God has made provision for us not to "fulfill the lust of the flesh," and we are responsible to follow His method of victory and living.

God speaks of these laws, or urges, as natures. One nature comes from our earthly fathers. We are born with it. When born naturally, we are "by nature children of wrath" (Eph. 2:3). People speak of someone and say, "That's just his nature," or, "That's just like him." Songs are written about "doing what comes naturally." Yes, it's natural to sin. "The wicked are estranged from the womb: they go astray as soon as they are born, speaking lies" (Ps. 58:3). When we are born again, we are partakers of the divine nature (see 2

Pet. 1:4). This is the nature of our heavenly Father. When a soul has been born of God, he has an inclination to live a godly life and to please his heavenly Father.

One part of him lusts for sin and selfish living. The other part longs for God and godly living. The flesh nature is dead to God but alive to sin. The Spirit nature is dead to sin but alive to God.

It is like a tug of war going on inside us all the time. God describes it like this: "For the flesh lusteth against the Spirit, and the Spirit against the flesh: and these are contrary the one to the other: so that ye cannot do the things that ye would" (Gal. 5:17). These two urges are ever present, though they may not be strongly operating at all times. The urge may be dormant but is stirred up by what we do. Whichever nature we feed the most is the one that is stronger.

I like to play golf, but I haven't played in months and hardly think about it. If I pass a golf course, though, the urge to play is stirred up. If I went out for eighteen holes and hit a few good shots, I would want to go again the next day. The same holds true about these natures. Whichever one is fed or stimulated by what we do, that is the one that will be the stronger. No wonder God said, "Set your affections on things above, not on things on the earth" (Col. 3:2). Here is a poem that says it well:

> Two natures beat within my breast,
>   One is foul, the other blest.
> The one I love, the one I hate—
>   The one I feed will dominate.*

Paul said, "Now if I do that I would not, it is no more I that do it, but sin that dwelleth in me" (Rom. 7:20). Sin is that law, that principle, working in me. Sin is the cause; sins are the effect. We need to get to the root of the problem. Too often we are only clipping the weeds in our lives instead of letting the Holy Spirit take control and uproot them. God said, "The Spirit indeed is willing, but the flesh is weak"

---

*Author unknown.

(Matt. 26:41). Oh, how weak the flesh is. You cannot put one ounce of confidence in it. We say, "I can handle it; it won't affect me." Then the flesh takes over, and down we go.

There are many incidents in the Bible that one could not understand apart from knowing that the old nature in man is struggling to get its way. Esau came in from working in the field, hungry and faint. He asked Jacob for something to eat. Jacob said, "Sell me this day thy birthright" (Gen. 25:31). Esau sold his most valuable possession, his rightful spiritual birthright, for a mess of pottage. Why did he do it? The old flesh just cries out to be satisfied, whether it is the hunger for food or for foolishness. The flesh is rotten. It lusts against the Spirit. It is powerful. The craving of the flesh has no end. A Christian must not feed it nor give in to it for one minute.

Probably the saddest record of the children of Israel is when they came out of bondage and began to give in to the flesh. Quickly they forgot about the bondage of Egypt and wanted to go back for the garlic, onions, and fish. They hated the manna that God provided. Finally, they came to Kadesh-Barnea. It was a land flowing with milk and honey. Instead of possessing the land, they voted not to enter the land. For forty years they wandered in circles until the last one of them had died in the wilderness. Their needs were met those years, and their shoes never wore out; but their lives were wasted!

Many believers today walk after the flesh and refuse to enter into what God has for them. They just sit year after year in someone's church, never contributing one thing spiritually to the cause of Christ. They wander and murmur, as did Israel, until they finally die. Oh, the wicked waste of life and influence. What makes them do it? That unbelieving sin nature within them.

WINNING THE WAR

Provision has been made that "sin shall not have dominion

over you" (Rom. 6:14). When Christ died, we died with him "that the body of sin might be destroyed, that henceforth we should not serve sin" (Rom. 6:6). Just as salvation is provided for all, but only operative for those who accept it, so deliverance from the power of sin is provided. The way for victory is told in Romans 6:11-13:

> Likewise reckon ye also yourselves to be dead indeed unto sin, but alive unto God through Jesus Christ our Lord. Let not sin therefore reign in your mortal body, that ye should obey it in the lusts thereof. Neither yield ye your members as instruments of unrighteousness unto sin: but yield yourselves unto God, as those that are alive from the dead.

Just count on it that this old urge to sin has been judged by God; reckon it to be so, and it will be so. This may sound paradoxical or it may sound simplistic, but bless God, it works. It works by faith, or God works it to be so in response to our faith in His promise that we are dead indeed to sin and now alive unto God. I can rebuke Satan, renounce the flesh, rely on the Holy Spirit, and see every thought brought into captivity to the obedience of Christ (2 Cor. 10:5).

Don't dwell on "being dead to sin" as much as you dwell on "being alive unto God." Count on it. Live it. Keep on the positive, and God will work in and through you. Then He gets the glory. It is not a struggle inside, whereby you suppress the flesh and you get the victory. If it were, you would soon glory in your victories and try to snatch the credit. Before you know it, you would fall again, for it is God who does it all, as we allow the Holy Spirit to do what He came to do.

A man was praying over and over, "O Lord, take the cobwebs out of our lives; remove the cobwebs." Finally another fellow cried out, "Lord, don't do it. Just kill the spider." Well, he wanted to get at the cause. We need to get at the cause of our sins and let the Holy Spirit take over so that we don't fulfil the lusts of the flesh.

Study Questions: Chapter 10

1. What is meant by the statement, "Every Christian is a schizophrenic"?
2. How did the apostle Paul describe this condition in Romans 7?
3. What is meant by "being dead unto sin"?
4. Discuss the truth of being alive unto God and how this "aliveness" is accomplished.

11
How on Earth Can I Overcome Temptation?

Temptation is not sin. Yielding to temptation is sin, but there is "a way to escape." Trials are not strange. It is our reaction to trials in the light of Scripture that is strange, because trials are "more precious than gold tried in the fire." Tribulation is sure. The world hates you, but "greater is he that is in you." Tricks of the devil are to be expected. We aren't ignorant of his devices, so know your enemy.

> Beloved, think it not strange concerning the fiery trial which is to try you, as though some strange thing happened unto you: But rejoice, inasmuch as ye are partakers of Christ's sufferings; that, when his glory shall be revealed, ye may be glad also with exceeding joy (1 Pet. 4:12,13).

Don't get shook up. Don't get excited. Don't strip your gears. Nothing unusual is happening; it is part of the training program. "Think it not strange." Count on it. Trials are coming as surely as night follows day. God has told us to expect trials. To give a person the impression that once he accepts Christ his trials are all over is a mistake. Usually trials just begin when Christ comes in. To repeat: It is not what happens to you that counts; it is your reaction that counts.

Trials come from above. They come from God. Trials are to bring out the best in us. They are for our good. They make us more usable. Temptation is from Satan. It is to bring out the bad in us, to destroy us, and to make us unusable. The trial of our faith is more precious than gold that is tried by fire (see 1 Pet. 1:7). Men work their hides off to pan for gold only to spend it or be robbed of it. How much more should a believer rejoice to pan for the gold of God that can never fade away or be stolen. Only as one looks at the things that are not seen and realizes that "our light affliction, which is but for a moment, worketh for us a far more exceeding and eternal weight of glory" (2 Cor. 4:17,18), can he know how to take and react to trials.

The way to react is to rejoice. Now, that's a new twist, isn't it? Rejoice. God is doing something wonderful, something great, for you. Right now He is molding and shaping you into the instrument He can use to His own glory. That airplane isn't going to be used until it has been tested. Steel has to be refined and tempered before it is usable. Soldiers have to be trained and prepared before being sent into combat. Trials should humble a Christian, for he should realize God must want to use him and make something out of him or else He would not put him through trials. "The fining pot is for silver, and the furnace for gold: but the Lord trieth the hearts" (Prov. 17:3). This should be a great encouragement to the child of faith and make him rejoice that God wants to use him.

Then the eternal future looks brighter because of the eternal weight of glory that shall be his "when his glory shall be revealed." It is an awful thing to be earthbound and time-conscious and not to be eternity-conscious.

Tribulations you can count on. "In the world ye shall have tribulation: but be of good cheer; I have overcome the world" (John 16:33). Tribulations are from without. Christians are in the world, but they are not of the world (see John 17:16). This whole world system is designed to defeat the Christian. Satan is in this world, and you can be sure he has placed a booby trap at every turn in the road.

"Marvel not, my brethren, if the world hate you" (1 John 3:13). Again, don't be shocked, don't be surprised at tribulations. You are in enemy territory. You are a threat. Your philosophies and ideas are contrary to its ways. The world cannot stand by and leave you alone. They hated your Leader. They crucified Him. If you are anything like Him, they will want to do the same to you.

The danger is for the believer to try to fit right in. The easy way out is to be "conformed to this world" until it can't tell the difference between a child of God and one of its own. No wonder God says, "Whosoever . . . will be a friend of the world is the enemy of God" (James 4:4). Whether or not we declare ourselves the enemies of this world, it is out to destroy us.

God's children must "love not the world, neither the things that are in the world" (1 John 2:15). The world just isn't going to love you. "If the world hate you, ye know that it hated me before it hated you. If ye were of the world, the world would love his own" (John 15:18,19). The world loves its own, and you know how they stick together. The Christian must be "blameless and harmless, the sons of God, without rebuke, in the midst of a crooked and perverse nation, among whom ye shine as lights in the world" (Phil. 2:15).

Yes, you can expect tribulations; but remember, "Greater is he that is in you, than he that is in the world" (1 John 4:4). The way to escape is to let the One who lives in you control you. The Holy Spirit will give you all the grace needed for victory.

COUNT IT ALL JOY

"My brethren, count it all joy when ye fall into divers temptations" (James 1:2). By faith that what God says is true, the child of God counts it all joy when he is surrounded by temptation. The word "fall into" is the same as that for the man who "fell among" thieves. He was surrounded. So often when it rains, it pours. Satan doesn't shoot one arrow, but many fiery darts. There are divers temptations, that is, many different kinds. When you feel you have one conquered, another five different temptations may be hurled at you.

It isn't a sin to be tempted. It's yielding to it that is sin. "Let no man say when he is tempted, I am tempted of God: for God cannot be tempted with evil, neither tempteth he any man: but every man is tempted, when he is drawn away of his own lust, and enticed" (James 1:13,14). God never tempts us. Temptation comes from within us. The old sin nature, that old urge to sin, is ever active. "The flesh lusteth

117

against the Spirit" (Gal. 5:17). "The heart is deceitful above all things, and desperately wicked" (Jer. 17:9). Not to realize this is to let down one's guard and be susceptible to every spiritual disease in the book.

THE TEMPTER

Then God says man is "enticed." This word means "to bait" or "lure out of safety." Satan baits us. He lures us out of safety until we stumble and yield to temptation. He waves temptations in front of our old sin nature, and we are drawn to sin.

"There hath no temptation taken you but such as is common to man: but God is faithful, who will not suffer you to be tempted above that ye are able; but will with the temptation also make a way to escape, that ye may be able to bear it" (1 Cor. 10:13). Three specific statements will help every Christian: First, all temptations are common to man. You are not alone. You are not being picked on. You cannot say, "No one knows what I have been through." You cannot say, "No one knows what it is like." Others have been through the same. It is common to man. Others have made it, and so can you.

Second, "God is faithful." He will not allow more than you can bear. There is no excuse for sinning. Don't say you can't take it. You can. God will not allow Satan to go beyond your strength. You can count on that. Too many want to excuse their sin and even blame God. You cannot do that.

And third, God assures "a way of escape, that ye may be able to bear it." He does not always keep us from temptation, but He promises to keep us through it, if we let Him. The way of escape will be dealt with at the end of this chapter. Make no mistake, there is a way of escape no matter what your besetting sin might be, but you must take that way yourself.

"You tricked me!" Yes, Satan is up to his old tricks, and God warns, "Put on the whole armor of God, that ye may be able to stand against the wiles of the devil" (Eph. 6:11).

He is a tricky rascal. You need to know your enemy. Satan is for real. The occult, the horoscopes, the ouiji boards, the fortune tellers, the church of Satan are all part of his masquerade. He wears many disguises. Don't be deceived or lulled to sleep by him. Even Michael, the archangel, recognized that the devil was not someone to be toyed with (Jude 9). Satan needs to be feared in the proper way.

A Roaring Lion

"Be sober, be vigilant; because your adversary the devil, as a roaring lion, walketh about, seeking whom he may devour" (1 Pet. 5:8). He is on the prowl. In the parked car, at the drive-in, at the dance, the devil shows up to trick young people into false romances and an ultimate loss of purity. Watching TV, playing cards, taking that social drink are often first steps to a ruined life. Beware, "lest Satan should get an advantage of us: for we are not ignorant of his devices" (2 Cor. 2:11). He wants to wreck your life. Satan is to be feared as a roaring lion. He will devour you in one great gulp if you play around the lion's den.

A Serpent

You had better fear him more as a serpent. "And the great dragon was cast out, that old serpent, called the Devil, and Satan, which deceiveth the whole world" (Rev. 12:9). He is a subtle serpent. He can easily slip around and deceive even believers. One of his chief methods of deceiving is to counterfeit the real thing. There is a counterfeit fun for the joy of the Lord. Some churches are nothing more than entertainment houses. There is no preaching and no conviction brought about through all that goes on Sunday after Sunday.

An Angel of Light

Satan should be feared as a roaring lion, he should be more feared as a serpent, but he should be most feared as an angel of light. Warning of false teachers, Paul said, "And no marvel; for Satan himself is transformed into an angel of light. Therefore it is no great thing if his ministers also be transformed as the ministers of righteousness; whose end shall be according to their works" (2 Cor. 11:14,15). This tells me that there are preachers in pulpits who are the servants of Satan appearing as the ministers of righteousness. If this were my own statement, I could expect deep resentment from some church members, but it is the Word of God. These poor preachers deny the blood of Christ and say the Bible is full of errors and myths. They tell people, "There is no hell," or, "Just do the best you can and all is well"; they are blind leaders of the blind, and a multitude "follow their pernicious ways" (2 Pet. 2:2) into a real and eternal hell.

Believers must be grounded in the Word of God and not be "carried about with every wind of doctrine, by the sleight of men, and cunning craftiness, whereby they lie in wait to deceive" (Eph. 4:14).

DEFEAT THE DEVIL

To defeat the devil one must recognize him. He is for real. He is after you. He is a formidable enemy. He is powerful, and he has an enormous fifth column of cohorts. "For we wrestle not against flesh and blood, but against principalities, against powers, against the rulers of the darkness of this world, against spiritual wickedness in high places" (Eph. 6:12).

The resources given by God to defeat the devil are "the whole armor of God." These are listed in Ephesians 6:13–17. Any earnest Christian who wants victory will keep a balanced Christian life and not neglect any of the armor.

"Resist the devil, and he will flee from you" (James 4:7). It works! It really does. Just as in verse 3 God says, "You have not because you ask not," so are many defeated simply because, by the power and authority given them, they simply have not resisted the devil. This has to be done as literally as one has to say literally, "I will," to be married. Not only that, but resisting the devil has to be done over and over and not just once for all.

One day as I was driving the thirty-nine miles from my home to Moody Bible Institute, I came under an attack from Satan and his demons. He flooded my mind with temptations and thoughts. I resisted him in Jesus' name and demanded he depart from me. Immediately he did. About two minutes later my mind and heart were attacked again. Once again I resisted him in Jesus' name and commanded him to leave. He did. Another minute or so passed, and the same attack broke out. It was weird. I felt the power of Satan as never before. This happened over and over for about thirty minutes. Finally he left me alone, and such an attack has never recurred in a way so concentrated and continuous. I learned from experience that Satan will flee, but we must resist him in Jesus' name.

Finally, one needs to rebuke him in Jesus' name and demand he depart. Jesus did it and so can we. Knowing that what Peter had just said was really provoked by Satan, Jesus said, "Get thee behind me, Satan" (Matt. 16:23). As children of the King, we too have the power and authority to rebuke Satan. I am convinced many Christians stumble and fall because they are uninformed about Satan and don't boldly rebuke him.

In that great and terrible day of the Lord, the Scripture declares, "They overcame him by the blood of the Lamb, and by the word of their testimony" (Rev. 12:11). If they can do it, so can we. Claim the blood. Dr. A. W. Tozer told how he claimed the blood of Christ for his new church. He walked all the way around it one day with his finger against the wall and rebuked Satan, telling him to stay out. Satan did leave, and some troubles that had arisen ended. When next Satan attacks, in Jesus' name claim the blood of Christ and rebuke Satan, driving him behind you.

MAKE IT ALL WORK

How do you make it all work? How do you come out the winner? How do you have victory in temptation or testing, in trials or tribulation?

It all starts with the right attitude. Attitudes precede and produce actions. If your attitudes are wrong, your actions will be wrong. If your attitudes are right, your actions will be right. No matter what the problem or predicament, whether it is testing or temptation, from God or Satan, I am to know that "all things work together for good to them that love God, to them who are the called according to his purpose" (Rom. 8:28). Knowing this and acting on it, I won't be bothered, nor will I become bitter. Whatever it is, I know it is for my good and God's glory. Oh, the thing happening may not be good itself. It may hurt. I may weep, but it is all working together for my good. I can count on that.

A second attitude is "in every thing give thanks: for this is the will of God in Christ Jesus concerning you" (1 Thess. 5:18). This attitude turns tragedy into triumph. It honors God. It proves one trusts that Romans 8:28 is true.

A healthy attitude is to say, "This is the day which the Lord hath made; we will rejoice and be glad in it" (Ps. 118:24). God did make it and plan it. The stars and planets are all still in place. He hasn't lost His power. He is in control. He planned this day and I can rejoice in it.

Another positive attitude to assume is "I can do all things through Christ which strengtheneth me" (Phil. 4:13). A Christian has no right to say, "I can't." One ought never to alibi, saying, "I just couldn't help it." Yes, he can; and by faith he should begin being positive and saying, "I can."

FOURFOLD FORMULA FOR VICTORY

"Walk in the Spirit, and ye shall not fulfil the lusts of the flesh" (Gal. 5:16). Make this a reality in your life and not a fantasy. Work at learning to walk as much as you did at learning to golf or hunt or bowl.

"Thy Word have I hid in mine heart, that I might not sin against thee" (Ps. 119:11). M & M candies are well known. When Roger Maris and Mickey Mantle played for the New York Yankees, they were a well-known and powerful "M & M" combination. The "M & M" for the Christian is *memorize* and *meditate* on the Word of God. Meditate on it, and you shall prosper (Josh. 1:8).

"Watch and pray, that ye enter not into temptation: the spirit indeed is willing, but the flesh is weak" (Matt. 26:41). Try the pray-as-you-go plan. Prayer taps all the resources and the power of God. We are admonished, "Let us therefore come boldly unto the throne of grace, that we may obtain mercy, and find grace to help in time of need" (Heb. 4:16). Here God tells us we can store up grace for a time when it is needed. This is preventive medicine. Most people could stand a good dose of grace daily.

"Be not overcome of evil, but overcome evil with good" (Rom. 12:21). Any sports fan or war strategist will tell you the best defense is a good offense. How true it is in the spiritual realm. You can be sure Satan isn't going to sit around, so you had better stay on the offensive. I've found that being so busy for God that you don't have time for an idle mind is a sure way to win. Look for ways to witness. Find things to do for the dear Lord. The devil just won't find an opening if your time is filled for the Lord.

Do you really want the victory? Do you really want to lay up treasures in glory? Do you really want to live a cut above those around you? Then work at it. You can be sure Satan works for your defeat.

Study Questions: Chapter 11

1. What is the difference between trials and temptations?
2. What should be the believer's reaction to trials? Why?
3. Discuss tribulations and their source.
4. Name the three beings under which Satan appears and the characteristics of each.
5. How is Satan to be defeated?
6. What is the fourfold formula for victory?

12
How on Earth Can I Grow Up Spiritually?

A baby is so cute and lovable, but to remain a baby five or twenty-five years would not be cute; it would be a disaster. God thinks this way about spiritual matters too. He says, "Grow in grace, and in the knowledge of our Lord and Savior Jesus Christ" (2 Pet. 3:18). Physical growth can be seen and enjoyed, and so can spiritual growth. When a person is "born again," he is a baby spiritually and needs to grow up. This is what the writer of Hebrews stressed in Hebrews 5:12–6:1:

> For when the time ye ought to be teachers, ye have need that one teach you again which be the first principles of the oracles of God; and are become such as have need of milk, and not of strong meat. For every one that useth milk is unskilful in the word of righteousness: for he is a babe. But strong meat belongeth to them that are of full age, even those who by reason of use have their senses exercised to discern both good and evil. Therefore leaving the principles of the doctrine of Christ, let us go on unto perfection. . . .

The word "perfection" is the same Greek word as the term "full age" in verse 14. It means "grown-up" or "mature." Too many Christians remain babes, thus the admonition. Others have their growth stunted and remain dwarfs. Some grow slowly and seem retarded spiritually. Others grow up and are of great service to God and His people.

A baby is one who still feeds on milk. It would be shocking to see a ten-year-old boy still taking a bottle. It is just as shocking to see ten-year-old Christians taking nothing but the "milk of the Word." A baby can't feed himself. Many Christians never learn to feed themselves on the Word of God. They don't study it or even read it. Babies can't walk by themselves or talk. They can't discern what is good for them. They would freely play with a sharp, shiny knife, unaware of its dangers. Babies have to be entertained much of the time. They are quite selfish, always wanting things. On and on we could go, and the parallels in the spiritual life are so obvious. It would be easy to identify individuals fitting every characteristic of a baby in the spiritual realm.

There is a difference between spirituality and spiritual maturity. The difference is like that of a five-year-old boy who is healthy and a five-year-old who is sickly. Maturity has to do with age and growth. Spirituality compares to the health of a person.

A person can be a ten-year-old Spirit-filled Christian walking in the Spirit, or he can be a ten-year-old carnal Christian walking in the flesh. This carnal Christian is the same age as the other, but spiritually ill. He may have one disease, or he may be a spiritual wreck with jealousy and anger and bitterness all at once in his life. Like boils, they poison the whole system.

It takes the cleansing of the blood of Christ to get one back into good health spiritually. This healing can be instantaneous upon confession of sin. Growth, though, takes time. It is a slow process, even as in the physical realm.

SPIRITUAL FOOD, EXERCISE, AND REST

In physical growth there are three important elements: food, exercise, and rest. These three have a parallel in the spiritual realm too: feeding on the Word, exercising in witnessing, and resting through prayer and worship.

The correlation between physical and spiritual growth is striking. The place of the Word of God is even more striking. In the physical realm birth is just phenomenal. In the spiritual realm God says, "Being born again, not of corruptible seed, but of incorruptible, by the Word of God, which liveth and abideth for ever" (1 Pet. 1:23). The Word of God is essential, for it is the incorruptible seed in the heart (see Luke 8:11). It also is the source of the faith that saves, for "faith cometh by hearing, and hearing by the Word of God" (Rom. 10:17). The Word is the milk for babies to grow on, for we are admonished, "As newborn babes, desire the sincere milk of the word, that ye may grow thereby" (1 Pet. 2:2). The first time I gave our baby son his bottle, this verse became alive as I saw him sucking on that bottle furiously. Oh, that today believers would feed so enthusiastically.

When our son was six months old, the doctor said we needed to vaccinate him. I said, "But it will hurt the baby!" He said, "You don't want him catching smallpox, do you?" Of course I didn't. So he was vaccinated. There is a spiritual vaccination with the Word as David said, "Thy word have I hid in mine heart, that I might not sin against Thee" (Ps. 119:11). The Word of God memorized and hidden away in the heart will surely keep one from sinning. Apply yourself wholly to the Scripture. The best place to keep the Bible is in your heart.

᾽ Babies need to learn to walk. You put them in a lighted place to walk. "Thy word is a lamp unto my feet, and a light unto my path" (Ps. 119:105). To learn to talk one needs instruction and understanding. "The entrance of thy words giveth light; it giveth understanding unto the simple" (Ps. 119:130). Children as they grow need to be taught to wash. God speaks of "the washing of water by the word" (Eph. 5:26). Jesus also said, "Now ye are clean through the word which I have spoken unto you" (John 15:3). Sometimes there is the need of an operation to cut out something harmful. "The word of God is quick, and powerful, and sharper than any twoedged sword, piercing even to the dividing asunder of soul and spirit, and of joints and marrow, and is a discerner of the thoughts and intents of the heart" (Heb. 4:12). It is as a sharp scalpel in the hands of the Great Physician.

There are many other uses of the Word, but just two more must attract our attention now. It is a phenomenon how couples begin to look alike after being married for years. "But we all, with open face beholding in a glass [the Word of God, James 1:23] the glory of the Lord, are changing into the same image from glory to glory even as by the Spirit of the Lord" (2 Cor. 3:18). Then there is a great vocation for the grown-up Christian to "preach the Word" (2 Tim. 4:2).

Great was the admonition of the pastor who said, "God has written you a letter, and brethren, you ought to read your mail." It is essential to spiritual growth. No wonder Job said, "I have esteemed the words of his mouth more than my necessary food" (Job 23:12). Jeremiah said, "Thy words were found, and I did eat them; and thy word was unto me the joy and rejoicing of mine heart" (Jer. 15:16).

Don't kill your appetite for the food of the soul by eating the garbage of the world. This is what is wrong with worldly amusements and habits. They kill your taste for the Word of God, until you will be like the children of Israel when they said, "Our soul loatheth this light bread" (Num. 21:5). Reading and meditating on the Scriptures is letting God speak to you.

Another spiritual factor in growth is prayer. This is you speaking to God. God hears prayer. You never get a busy signal. Prayer changes things. It also changes you. When Moses came off the mount from talking with God, his face shone with a radiance not seen before (see Exod. 34:29,30). One reason some Christians radiate the glory and joy of the Lord is that they spend time in His presence in prayer talking things over with Him.

What is prayer? It is just talking to God as you would to your best friend. You don't need to try to impress God with profound words; just talk to Him. Tell Him all about it. What are your needs? "Let your requests be made known unto God. And the peace of God, which passeth all understanding, shall keep your hearts and minds through Christ Jesus" (Phil. 4:6,7).

Why pray? To get things from God. "Ye have not, because ye ask not" (James 4:2). "Ask, and it shall be given you" (Matt. 7:7). Jesus said we are to pray, "Give us this day our daily bread" (Matt. 6:11). Don't take your needs for granted. You never test the resources of God until you pray for the impossible.

We find God's will for our lives by prayer. Paul prayed, "Lord, what wilt thou have me to do?" (Acts 9:6). Do you know God's will for your career? For your companion? Then ask Him about it. You have not because you ask not!

When to pray? The psalmist said, "O Lord, in the morning will I direct my prayer unto thee, and will look up" (Ps. 5:3). That is the way to start the day. Again, the psalmist said, "Evening, and morning, and at noon, will I pray, and cry aloud: and he shall hear my voice" (Ps. 55:17). In other words, "Pray without ceasing" (1 Thess. 5:17). A Christian ought so to talk with God that he is conscious of God's presence at all times and carries on a continuous conversation with Him about everything.

How do you pray? "The effectual fervent prayer of a righteous man availeth much" (James 5:16). Prayer should not be idle mumbling. It should not be emotional blabbering. One should be aware of being in the presence of a holy God at the throne of grace (see Heb. 4:16). Hannah said, "I . . . have poured out my soul before the Lord" (1 Sam. 1:15), and God gave her a child when she had been unable to have children. Get serious about praying. Don't be like a little child in a toy store saying, "Give me this" or "I want that."

A third spiritual exercise for growth is witnessing. The Dead Sea always takes in and never gives out. It is stagnant. Nothing lives in it. A Christian who constantly takes in and never witnesses will be stagnant. It will certainly stunt his growth. Every saved person this side of heaven ought to be vitally concerned about every lost person this side of hell.

One thing that distinctly characterized the early church was witnessing. They flexed their spiritual muscles and "went everywhere preaching the word" (Acts 8:4). They were persecuted, put in jail, but how they grew in number and in stature! When persecuted they prayed, "And now, Lord, behold their threatenings: and grant unto thy servants, that with all boldness they may speak thy word, . . . and when they had prayed, the place was shaken where they were assembled together; and they were all filled with the Holy Ghost, and they spake the word of God with boldness" (Acts 4:29–31).

Study Questions: Chapter 12

1. Describe spiritual babes.
2. What is the difference between spirituality and spiritual growth?
3. In what ways does the Word of God effect spiritual growth?
4. Discuss the role of prayer in spiritual growth.

13
What on Earth Are the Gifts and Callings?

What is a spiritual gift? Dr. C. C. Ryrie said, "A spiritual gift is a God-given ability for service." Dr. Leslie B. Flynn said, "A gift is a Spirit-given ability for Christian service." It is almost universally agreed that gifts are abilities for spiritual service and not natural talents. There is a difference. Many will often call natural talents "gifts" and speak of the person as being "gifted" when the person may not even be a Christian and his abilities have nothing to do with Christian service. A Christian needs to be discerning about using terms in a scriptural way but be aware others may not use them so.

A good example is a beautiful solo voice. It can be used in a night club or for Christian service, but it is nowhere spoken of as a "gift." This distinction should be kept clear in one's thinking.

Another distinction that is often overlooked is the difference between gifts and callings. God indicates a difference when He states "the gifts and callings of God are without repentance" (Rom. 11:29). What is the difference between the two? The *gift* is a Spirit-given ability while the *calling* is the position or office of service where one uses his gifts. In Ephesians 4:11 there is a list of offices or callings. These are in reality not gifts but callings of individuals. The footnote on Ephesians 4:11 in the Scofield Bible says it so well:

In 1 Corinthians 12:8–28, the Spirit is seen as enduing the members of the body of Christ with spiritual gifts, or enablements for a varied service; here certain Spirit-endued men, viz. apostles, prophets, evangelists, pastors, and teachers, are themselves the gifts whom the glorified Christ bestows upon His body, the church. In Corinthians the gifts are spiritual enablements for specific service; in Ephesians the gifts are men who have such enablements.

There is no gift of apostling. Paul was "an apostle of Jesus Christ by the will of God, to the saints which are at Ephesus" (Eph. 1:1). First Corinthians 1:1 states, "Paul, called to be an apostle of Jesus Christ through the will of God." Paul was called to be an apostle, not given a gift of apostling. A man today declares he is called to be a pastor. He has gifts that enable him to do all a pastor should do. He must have a gift of teaching, be "apt to teach" (1 Tim. 3:2), to qualify as a pastor, but there just is no gift of pastoring. It is a calling and should be regarded as such and not be called a gift.

One difference in a gift and a calling seems to be that a "calling" is a position of full-time service. That is to say, a person is to live by that service. Chapter 9 of 1 Corinthians goes into detail to say this very thing. Paul indicates that as an apostle he has the right to expect to be supported by them. Then he sums up Christian calling and service, saying, "Even so hath the Lord ordained that they which preach the gospel should live of the gospel" (1 Cor. 9:14).

There are those who are "called to teach." These live by their teaching. Many who teach Sunday school or Bible classes have a gift of teaching, but it is not the source of their livelihood. It so happens that in this case there is a gift of teaching as well as a calling to teach, and one can have the gift of teaching but make his living in some other vocation. This is perfectly understandable by all today. The distinction between a gift and a calling to teach is quite obvious.

Men are called to be evangelists today. This is a definite calling and scriptural office, even though in the past such an office fell into disrepute because of misuse. Those called of God to be evangelists are to live by that calling as well. Billy Graham, John R. Rice, D. L. Moody, and Billy Sunday, to name a few, are valid examples of the scriptural calling of evangelists.

Now, notice carefully, there is no gift of evangelism named as well as the calling of evangelists, as in the case of teaching. This distinction has wide implications. Pastors have excused their lack of evangelistic efforts and effectiveness by saying they did not have the gift of evangelism. The truth is that every Christian is to be a witness. The ultimate aim of the Great Commission that every pastor and church must heed is to get the gospel to every creature. This is not a mandate for missionaries overseas but for Christians everywhere. Not only that, but all pastors are under the injunction to "do the work of an evangelist" (2 Tim. 4:5).

A prevalent concept of the office of pastor-teacher that negates any personal responsibility of the pastor to witness is unscriptural and detrimental. A pastor is to build up "the saints for the work of the ministry," but this does not at all mean an exemption from a pastor's responsibility to be an example to his people in witnessing, as well as in Bible study and prayer.

Because of false teaching on the "gift of evangelism," many Christians have been lulled into feeling no responsibility to witness. Some deliberately hide behind the guise of not having a "gift of evangelism" as an excuse not to witness. Untold harm has come to the cause of Christ because of false teaching about a gift of evangelism. There just is not a gift of evangelism named in Romans 12 and 1 Corinthians 12, which list the gifts of the Spirit. If every Christian witnessed today as every Christian did in the book of Acts, we just might turn the world upside down again, or would it be turned right side up!

One more important fact should be noted about gifts. To be scripturally correct in saying someone has a particular spiritual gift, it seems one should have an unusual ability to perform such gifts. To illustrate, consider giving. Every Christian gives, but every Christian doesn't have the gift of giving. The same is true about faith. Every Christian is to exercise faith, but every Christian doesn't have the gift of faith.

Let's look at the individual gifts as listed, and see how this premise fits the overall teaching. The gifts can be divided several ways. We shall consider them in alphabetical order under speaking gifts, serving gifts, and sign gifts.

SPEAKING GIFTS

Exhortation

Paul speaks of having "gifts differing according to the grace that is given us," and says that each should give

133

himself to the gift that is entrusted to his use, such as, "He that exhorteth, [wait] on exhortation" (Rom. 12:8). The Greek words for "exhortation" here are another form of the Greek word used for the Holy Spirit in John 14:16, when He is said to be another "Comforter." To exhort really had two ideas behind it: "to encourage or comfort, and to admonish."

Every believer is to "exhort one another daily, while it is called today; lest any of you be hardened through the deceitfulness of sin" (Heb. 3:13). This surely does not mean every Christian has the "gift of exhortation," but every Christian can encourage others; in fact, Christians are under obligation to do so, just as every Christian is to give whether or not he has the gift of giving.

This, then, seems to indicate that to have the gift of exhortation is a matter of degree of ability. One who has the gift of exhortation has a great degree of ability to encourage others. It seems to be a natural thing to do without any special effort at all. One with this gift in the ministry encourages and challenges his people in the work of the Lord. His ministry has a great effect to excite others to serve the Lord. Dr. Jerry Falwell, pastor of the Thomas Road Baptist Church in Lynchburg, Virginia, who is seen by millions on television, obviously has the gift of exhortation. His messages are saturated with comfort and encouragement. Being associated with him, traveling with him, and listening to him hundreds of times, I find it evident that Dr. Falwell makes people around him want to do more than they ever dreamed they could do.

The need for exhortation is great, as seen by the admonition to "exhort one another daily, lest any be hardened through the deceitfulness of sin." Christians need exhorting daily. Once a week on Sunday is not enough. Exhortation is a preventive from being "hardened through the deceitfulness of sin." If all Christians realized the absolute necessity of their duty in the body of Christ to exhort others *daily,* they could revolutionize churches. Christians sharing with others their own blessings and answers to prayer and fresh illuminations from the Word are simple ways to encourage others. A word fitly spoken does so much.

A fellow student in a college said to me one night almost as a passing remark that he believed God was going to use my life, and he felt I had potential to be a real blessing. This had a profound effect on my whole life. I have discovered that people are starved for a little encouragement. How easy it is to forget yourself and look for an opportunity to say something encouraging; it is one of the most rewarding things you can ever do.

Knowledge and Wisdom

"For to one is given by the Spirit the word of wisdom; to another the word of knowledge by the same Spirit" (1 Cor. 12:8) is the way the gifts of wisdom and knowledge are introduced. There is surely a close connection between the two. The gift of knowledge has to do with knowledge and understanding the revealed truth in the Word of God. Wisdom is the ability to apply the spiritual truth to practical living. Both of these gifts are important for those who minister by teaching and preaching.

It is important to note that every Christian is to "grow in grace, and in the knowledge of our Lord and Savior Jesus Christ" (2 Pet. 3:18). As one studies the Word of God in dependence on the ultimate teacher of the Word, the Holy Spirit, he can gain more and more knowledge, but there are those who just have a knack, an unusual ability, to grasp the truths of the Word and fit it all together. This is the gift of knowledge. The ability to communicate it to others in an understandable manner is the gift of teaching. This gift of knowledge can be discovered as one reads the Bible and begins to find that the truths of God's Word just open up to him. His understanding of verse after verse and truth after truth will be clear and logical.

This gift is obvious in the great theologians and writers who have elucidated the great truths of the Bible. The ability of men to systematize and pull together Scripture and the doctrines of the Bible is a gift with which God has endowed many for the edifying of the body of Christ.

The gift of wisdom seems to be used especially in counseling. Some have the ability, as did Solomon, to hear a person's problem and come up with a scriptural understanding and solution that is of great help to the individual. We had a man in our church who seemed to have an uncanny ability to sit in board meetings, hear a matter out, see through the problem, and come up with a solution that would amaze us all. He had the gift of wisdom. In another church, a lady had great wisdom in counseling and was a help to many younger women in our church. She, too, had the gift of wisdom.

Prophecy

The "gift of prophecy" is a much-used expression today. How it is used contemporarily is not necessarily the biblical use of the word. Today, prophesying is commonly identified with the action of predicting the future. There is an enormous interest in the future and in foretelling the future. In the Old Testament the prophets did foretell the future—quite often in vivid detail.

The gift of prophecy as mentioned in Romans 12:6 and 1 Corinthians 14:5 is taken by most Bible scholars to refer to forthtelling and not foretelling. Dr. Kenneth Gangel says, "The gift of prophecy is congregational preaching that explains and applies God's revelation." This seems to be what most conservative theologians believe prophecy meant in New Testament times.

The use of this gift, as well as all others (though this one is mentioned specially), must be done in love, or it profits nothing (1 Cor. 13:2,3). Preaching is not to be used to whip people from the pulpit. Preaching has two basic functions: One is to reach the sinner, to evangelize the sinner; the other is to teach the saint, to edify the saint. Romans 10:13,14 makes this point clear: "For whosoever shall call upon the name of the Lord shall be saved. How then shall they call on him in whom they have not believed? and how shall they believe in him of whom they have not heard? and how shall they hear without a preacher?"

From this, only one conclusion can be made: God expects preachers to preach the gospel and people to be saved as an immediate result of gospel preaching. First Corinthians 1:18–21 bears out this same fact and concludes with the glorious statement, "It pleased God by the foolishness of preaching to save them that believe." Indeed, the Bible emphasizes witnessing by the one-to-one method, but alongside that is the emphasis of evangelistic preaching to reach the masses.

Some have said the church is not to reach the sinner but to feed the sheep and send them out for the lost. To be sure, the saints need to be fed and led out to witness, but Paul expected the lost to come to church, hear the preaching, and be convicted and converted right there. This fact is overlooked by some godly men today.

Notice carefully 1 Corinthians 14:23–25:

> If therefore the whole church be come together into one place, and all speak with tongues, and there come in those that are unlearned, or unbelievers, will they not say that ye are mad? But if all prophesy, and there come in one that believeth not, or one unlearned, he is convinced of all, he is judged of all: And thus are the secrets of his heart made manifest; and so falling down on his face, he will worship God.

What a packed passage. First, it is speaking about a church meeting when the people of God are gathered into "one place." Unbelievers are expected to be there, contrary to what some may expect today. Through the preaching, they are expected to be convicted and converted. Should a preacher expect any less today? Once when this passage was read to a pastor who took the extreme view that the church was not the place to preach the gospel to get people saved, he burst into tears and said to me, "I've been so wrong." His ministry was transformed, as well as his church, as people began to be saved in their Sunday service. Seeing babes born is one of the most beautiful sights and edifying experiences any believer ever encounters.

The second purpose, and equally important, is to teach and edify the saint. This is emphasized in the same fourteenth chapter of 1 Corinthians in verses 3,4,5,12,17, and 26. God declares that "he that prophesieth speaketh unto men to edification, and exhortation, and comfort" (v. 3). Prophesying is speaking to men.

One purpose given here is to edify, to build up the saint. It is a terrible tragedy to major in evangelism to the extent that a church is filled with runts, dwarfs, pygmies, and babes because there just is not enough feeding and nourishing of the saints. Either extreme, evangelism with no teaching, or teaching with no reaching of the lost, is a warped and unscriptural ministry. The church is for both, and both are to be done through preaching as well.

What about women? They can have the gift of prophesying. According to Acts 21:9, Philip's daughter prophesied. You can be sure they did not violate the teaching or order of God by speaking in a church, "for it is a shame for women to speak in the church" (1 Cor. 14:35). Also, you can be sure they did not teach nor preach to men, for a woman is not "to teach, nor to usurp authority over the man" (1 Tim. 2:12).

No, I'm not a male chauvinist, and neither was Paul. God has His order, and He made each for specific purposes. No man should cry because he cannot bear a baby, and no woman should cringe because she does. An airplane is for flying in the air, not for floating on the ocean. God has not given His decree in the Word of God and then countermanded his orders by calling women to pastor today. He is the same today as He was two thousand years ago. Our society is in a mess today because men are not functioning as the heads of homes, as the spiritual leaders, and because women have "come a long way" downhill until femininity, ladylikeness, and the fragrance of their loveliness is lost. God help us.

My wife prophesies, but only before women in Bible classes, Sunday school, retreats for women, and women's clubs. She has her own ministry but is first a godly wife and mother. She has never felt deprived but totally fulfilled in bearing and rearing five wonderful children and being the greatest helpmeet to me and my ministry. We have no rivalry but are "heirs together of the grace of life" (1 Pet. 3:7), and thus get our prayers answered.

One who has the gift of prophesying should be careful to develop and dispense that gift. It is gratifying, having been teaching in Christian colleges for fifteen years, to see the transformation in preachers as they take courses in speech and homiletics. It is also grating to see someone (obviously called of God) stumble and fumble through a sermon when a little training could do so much to help him communicate effectively.

Often the question is asked, "How does one get to preach?" A simple solution is to buy up every little opportunity, and the larger ones will open when God knows you have been faithful in the little things. Too many fellows in schools want to preach in the First Church, but they aren't willing to preach first at the old people's home or the rescue mission. That is where most of us got our feet wet. These are excellent places to discern if one has the gift of prophecy.

Teaching

One of the terrible tragedies in a church is to give a sincere man or woman a Sunday school class of ten-year-olds when that person doesn't possess the gift of teaching. To teach in a Sunday school or a seminary, one must have the gift of teaching. The only difference in the two situations is that in the latter, one has the calling to teach as well as the gift of teaching, and thus scripturally earns his living by teaching in a seminary.

The gift of teaching is that special ability from the Lord to explain effectively and clearly and teach the Word of God. Many can teach effectively in a public school but have not the ability to teach spiritual truth from the Word of God. They might be able to memorize many facts about the Bible and give them faithfully but not have the gift of teaching. Years ago on the TV program "The $64,000 Question," some people answered many questions about the Bible, such as the names of the apostles, places, and events, but may not have had any perception of real spiritual truth. The gift of teaching will produce spiritual results and blessing in the lives of hearers, not just transfer facts. Real teaching transforms and does not just inform.

One who discerns he has that special ability to teach and explain spiritual insight into the Word of God should then "study to shew thyself approved unto God, a workman that needeth not to be ashamed, rightly dividing the word of truth" (1 Tim. 2:15). He should go to Bible school or seminary or take correspondence courses to prepare himself.

Then he should use that gift with individuals privately and with others publicly. This gift cannot be worn out, but it is sharpened "by reason of use." God declares:

> For when for the time ye ought to be teachers, ye have need that one teach you again which be the first principles of the oracles of God; and are become such as have need of milk, and not of strong meat. For every one that useth milk is unskilful in the word of righteousness: for he is a babe. But strong meat belongeth to them that are of full age, even those who by reason of use have their senses exercised to discern both good and evil (Heb. 5:12–14).

A word of warning is in order. God says, "My brother, be not many masters ["teachers" in Greek], knowing that we shall receive the greater judgment." Remember how Jesus scathingly warned about the "blind leaders of the blind" (Matt. 15:14). Someone said, "It is a sin to make the Word of God boring." It is just too easy to become mechanical and life-less, even deadening, when one teaches year after year. There will be more to answer for by such individuals, for there is an awesome responsibility in teaching.

SERVING GIFTS

The next set of gifts is sometimes called the serving gifts. This is not to imply that they are of less importance. As a matter of fact, one is the gift of government or ruling. We shall look at it first.

Government

This is a gift (1 Cor. 12:28) of ruling or leadership in the church. It is not a domineering dictatorship but a loving leadership; but make no mistake, it is a gift of ruling or directing in the work of God. Some have so emphasized that pastors are ministers and thus servants that they have missed an obvious fact. Paul declared himself a servant, but a "servant of Jesus Christ" (Rom. 1:1; Phil. 1:1). James did the same (James 1:1), as did Peter (2 Pet. 1:1), Jude (1), and John (Rev. 1:1). It is one thing to be a "bond slave" to Jesus Christ, but entirely unscriptural for a pastor with the gift of ruling to be bound by deacons and people so as to be unable to be led by the Spirit and exercise his gift. Likewise it is not of God for a pastor to run roughshod over his people until the whole church is angry and the work of God is in shambles.

Sheep need a shepherd, a leader. The most common characteristic of sheep is to go astray (Isa. 53:6). Three times in Hebrews 13, verses 7, 17, and 24, God speaks of those who "have the rule over you." They are to be remembered, obeyed, and saluted. God sets up the chain of command among His people and gives some this gift of ruling. It is not a place of prestige but of awesome responsibility, for they "must watch for your souls as they that must give an account" either with joy or grief. What an enormous weight must be on a surgeon who performs a delicate heart transplant! But that is just child's play compared to giving someone a new heart in Christ Jesus. The surgeon's results are dealing only with physical, temporal life, while the pastor is dealing with spiritual, eternal life.

A ship certainly needs a "helmsman." This is the meaning of the Greek word in 1 Corinthians 12:28 that is translated "government." The old ship of Zion needs God-appointed "helmsmen." Where in the world is the average church headed? Just as there is a desperate need of leadership in the political world, there is a great need of spiritual leadership in the Christian world. Many preachers have no vision or goal for their churches. Most have forgotten or forsaken the primary purpose of the church, that of the Great Commission to get the gospel to every creature (see Mark 16:15).

The work of God needs those to "preside" over the house of God to accomplish all that God intended. This is the idea of the word "rule" in Romans 12:8. Someone has to organize, train, and direct the work of God. Those with this gift do just that.

Other areas in the work of God where one can exercise

the gift of government or ruling include Sunday school super-intendents, trustees, and deacons who have appointed respon-sibilities in the church. Deacons were chosen as servants to wait on tables so that the pastor could carry out his ministry of the spiritual things. Deacons did not run Paul, that's for sure! It is unscriptural for board members to run churches so that the pastor cannot even invite a man to preach for him without the board approving it.

Discernment

The gift of discernment (1 Cor. 12:10) is possessed probably by theologians in particular. The Greek word for "discernment," *diakrisis,* comes from two Greek words, *dia* and *krino. Krino* means "to judge or discern" and is found in 1 Corinthians 2:15, where it tells of the spiritual man being discerned of no man. The world just doesn't under-stand him. Then the preposition *dia* in the Greek intensifies the word it connects and could mean "thoroughly." One with this gift, then, has a deep discernment or judgment of the spirits of men and spiritual things. He can sense truth from error. With this gift, one can see through phony people and false doctrine.

Every believer is to "try the spirits whether they are of God: because many false prophets are gone out into the world" (1 John 4:1). There is gullibility on the part of many to take anyone in or accept anything with the tag of Christianity on it. Not so according to Scripture. Some, like the Bereans, "search the Scripture" and try to discern whether or not it be of God. "Judge not, that ye be not judged" (Matt. 7:1) has been terribly misused. Judging is at-tacking another's motives and old-fashioned fault-finding. Discernment is being able to sense whether or not a person or a proposition is scriptural.

With the rise of hundreds of churches, many with only the vaguest attachment to the Lord Jesus or His Word, there is a great need for a gift of discernment. Then with the occultists and horoscopists who claim revelation from God, and those with ESP who claim religious overtones, these spirits also need to be tried. Many believe there is a great evidence of demon possession that is quite new in the United States. Also, the gift of discernment needs to be exercised in the charismatic movement. There is just too much difference doctrinally today. All cannot be of God! This gift needs to be heeded, lest people be "led captive" in these last days.

Paul told a preacher of old, Timothy, "that in the last days perilous times shall come," and there would be men "having a form of godliness, but denying the power thereof: from such turn away. For of this sort are they which creep into houses, and lead captive silly women laden with sins, led away with divers lusts, ever learning, and never able to come to the knowledge of the truth. Now as Jannes and Jambres withstood Moses, so do these also resist the truth: men of corrupt minds, reprobate concerning the faith" (2 Tim. 3:5–8).

What is it to have a "form of godliness, but [deny] the power thereof"? Two verses, 1 Timothy 3:16 and Romans 1:16, together seem to lay a foundation for true godliness. First Timothy 3:16 says, "And without controversy great is the mystery of godliness: God was manifest in the flesh, justified in the Spirit, seen of angels, preached unto the Gentiles, believed on in the world, received up into glory." Then Paul says, "I am not ashamed of the gospel of Christ: for it is the power of God unto salvation to every one that believeth" (Rom. 1:16). Two fundamental, essential things appear here. First, that the Lord Jesus Christ is not one whit less than "God manifest in the flesh." Anyone who denies this is not of God but is an Antichrist, according to 1 John 2:22,23; 4:1-3. And second, that the vicarious death, burial, and resurrection of the Lord Jesus Christ is the "power of God unto salvation." To deny this is to deny the "power" of godliness. The discerning of spirits must not be on the basis of "experiences" but on the expressed truth of the Word of God.

Faith

The gift of "serving faith" is different from the gift of "saving faith." According to Ephesians 2:8, it is taken that saving faith is "the gift of God." But this gift of faith in 1 Corinthians 12:9 has nothing to do with one's salvation but only his service. This is a special gift to members of the body of Christ for the work of Christ through His church (see Eph. 1:22,23).

Every Christian has faith, for "without faith it is impossible to please [God]" (Heb. 11:6). One's faith can be increased (Luke 17:5). Every believer can see "great and mighty things" done in answer to the "prayer of faith." It does not take the gift of faith to see miracles of provision and protection in answer to prayers of faith. Thousands of young people in schools see God provide for their needs over and over again in answer to prayer as they go through school on faith.

I saw the dear Lord do it many times while I was in school. Once I owed a board bill of thirty dollars that was due the Tuesday after Easter. I didn't have a penny toward it. The day before Easter I spent a season in prayer for that need. God gave me peace that he would supply the need. On Monday I received an Easter card from a couple with whom I had never corresponded—before or since. With the card was a brief note: "God laid it on our hearts to send you this." Enclosed was a check for thirty dollars.

George Mueller had the gift of faith and ran an orphanage in England for years on faith. Missionaries have gone to the mission field on faith and God has provided for their needs in miraculous ways. These have had the gift of faith. Perhaps some have tried to live the same way and run into disaster because they did not have the gift of faith. Many Christian ministries have prospered in fabulous ways because someone had the gift of faith. Others have failed because some very sincere Christian tried to do the same but did not have the same gift. I have seen too many students in Christian schools face disaster because someone challenged them to just "trust God," quit a job, and live by faith, when they too didn't have the gift of faith.

One should exercise all the faith he has in prayer, expecting God to answer and do miracles. If he does see God giving him that unusual faith to believe and expect miracles—great! Pray more, believe more, attempt more. But if one does not see continuous miracles and working of God in answer to faith, it may be he doesn't have this gift and should not become discouraged about it.

Giving

Every Christian should give. "It is more blessed to give than to receive" (Acts 20:35). Every Christian should not give his last dollar of savings, though, and expect God to multiply it back to him. Again, I've seen sincere, eager Christians deeply hurt because they tried to exercise a gift they did not have.

A dear friend of mine has the gift of giving. He gives away his money as if it were going out of style. Hundreds of seminary students have made it through school because this man has invested hundreds of thousands of dollars to help them prepare for the ministry. This man is wise and shrewd, and though he himself has had little formal education, he is a millionaire. He had the gift of giving and exercised it greatly long before he ever became a millionaire. For over twenty years I've known him to be generous. It has often been an inward longing of mine to be able to give so generously. On occasions I've given very liberally, but God has never multiplied my resources so that I could give like my friend does. I just don't have the gift of giving.

Every Christian can have the joy of giving and be blessed immensely, even financially, without the gift of giving. Let him be sure, though, that he has the gift of giving before he gives away his grocery money or house payments and expects God to double his returns!

Many dear saints of God have the gift of giving and exercise it regularly with relatively small amounts of money. Their gifts are noted, even as the widow's mite.

What if everyone had the gift of giving? If it is "more blessed to give than to receive" and "God loves a cheerful giver," then shouldn't more seek the gift of giving? Many would discover that they have the gift of giving if they would begin giving extra to God's work.

But God says, "He that giveth, let him do it with simplicity" (Rom. 12:8). It should not be done to be seen of men or to receive their praise, or there will be no future reward. The present praise will be the total reward. Give so that even your left hand doesn't know what your right hand does.

Another important fact seems to be that giving should be "distributing to the necessity of saints" (Rom. 12:13). Giving is specifically to care for the saints, and the Christian church is not solely responsible for feeding the starving world. No way in the world could it. This is not to say Christians should ignore the hungry and have no compassion, but it is dead wrong to bring guilt on Christians or the church because multitudes are starving. Many are starving because of their godless rejection of Christ and Christianity.

Helps

Everyone can help others, but some people have a real knack for being in the right place at the right time to help someone. Over and over I've seen people in churches become a pastor's right-hand man and have a fabulous ministry in helping out around the church. In one church where I've preached many times, a retired businessman always picks me up at the airport. He is a chauffeur for all visiting speakers. He runs errands and helps in so many ways. It is a delight to be around him and see the joy he has in helping in the work of the Lord. His reward will be great in heaven.

That person with the one talent who never put it to use but hid it troubles me. Could it be that someone with a gift that is not prominent might feel useless and not put to use the gift of helps because he doesn't get enough praise? To him who has put to use what God has given him shall be given more!

Showing Mercy

Dr. Jack Hyles closes his radio broadcast with the admonition, "Be kind to someone today; everyone has problems." Today there is a great need for the art of "showing mercy." This gift is like a rare orchid in beauty and is as fragrant as the sweetest flower in bloom. Romans 12:8 says, "He that sheweth mercy, [let him do it] with cheerfulness."

When I was a young and inexperienced pastor, a man whom

146

I knew committed suicide, and I was called at five in the morning to go to his home. The man's wife asked me to awaken their thirteen-year-old son and tell him about his father. A lady from our church who had the gift of mercy was already at the home, and I asked her to go with me to the boy. In a beautiful way, she sensed my need and took over. She woke the boy and told him the bad news with compassion and gentleness and tried to ease the pain. Showing mercy was one of her gifts, and she exercised it daily with people in our church.

Showing mercy is to be done "with cheerfulness," and it is not a doleful experience of feeling sorry for someone. Everyone should be "kind one to another" (Eph. 4:32), but some have a gift that excels this admonition.

SIGN GIFTS

The sign gifts are the gifts of healing, miracles, tongues, and interpretation of tongues. These are called sign gifts because they are spoken of as "signs" in Scripture.

Doubting Thomas did not believe that the Lord was risen from the dead. He needed proof. He said he would not believe unless he saw the nailprints in His hands (see John 20:25). When Thomas saw the nailprints, he believed and cried out, "My Lord and my God" (John 20:28). The nailprints are specifically called a sign, as the Word says, "And many other signs truly did Jesus in the presence of his disciples, which are not written in this book: but these are written, that ye might believe that Jesus is the Christ, the Son of God; and that believing ye might have life through his name" (John 20:30,31). The miracles Jesus performed were signs that people might believe—not as a display to satisfy curiosity, not as devotion to God, and not as a demonstration only of the power of God.

Tongues

"Tongues are for a sign" (1 Cor. 14:22, italics mine) as well. Not for a display of devotion, dedication, or discipleship, but for a sign, say the Scriptures. Whatever is done in

the church should be to convince the unbeliever so that "he will worship God" (1 Cor. 14:25). If there is no interpreter so that tongues can't be used to convince unbelievers, God says, "Let him keep silence in the church" (v. 28). Signs are stated outright as approval from God concerning the Lord Jesus; Scripture states, "A man approved of God among you by miracles and wonders and signs, which God did by him in the midst of you" (Acts 2:22). The apostles were confirmed by signs; 2 Corinthians 12:12 tells, "Truly the signs of an apostle were wrought among you in all patience, in signs, and wonders, and mighty deeds."

The question now is not, "Could God still give the sign gifts?" but, "Does He need to and desire to?" There is no question but that God can still do anything, even create a new world. This will be an oversimplification to some, but signs and miracles were so that men "might believe" (John 20:31). God declares, since His Word has been given and is complete, that "faith cometh by hearing, and hearing by the word of God" (Rom. 10:17). There is no need for the sign gifts when we have His Word.

The Lord Jesus said, "An evil and adulterous generation seeketh after a sign: and there shall no sign be given to it, but the sign of the prophet Jonas" (Matt. 12:39). Many believe the greatest signs anyone can want in his ministry are people being "born of God," whether through the preaching of the Word of God to the multitudes, as on the day of Pentecost when three thousand were converted, or through preaching Christ to only one as Philip did in Acts 8:35 when the eunuch was transformed. The greatest sign anyone can see is the transformation of someone like the woman at the well in John 4. Many Samaritans believed in Christ because of this woman (v. 39).

It is not the purpose of this book nor this chapter to prove anything about a few of the more spectacular gifts. The purpose is to inform God's people about the ministry of the Holy Spirit to carry out the Great Commission so that we might line up with the Lord, who said, "I will build my church" (Matt. 16:18). For a detailed study, get Leslie Flynn's book, *19 Gifts of the Spirit*. Let us look now at the rest of the gifts.

Healing

Cancer is frightening. No one wants to be sick. Good health is a deep desire of everyone. People will try anything, do anything, and give anything to be cured.

Over and over people ask me, "Do you believe in divine healing?" Emphatically I say, "Yes!" God healed my son of epilepsy when doctor after doctor said that he would have epilepsy for the rest of his life!

Again I am asked, "Do you believe people have the gift of healing today?" No, I don't. The gift of healing was given to the Twelve in Matthew 10. In Matthew 17 they were not able to heal a man's son; and when they asked the Lord why, He answered, "Because of your unbelief" (v. 20). Have you ever heard a "healer" take the responsibility for not healing someone? No, the fault is always with the one who was not healed because of his lack of faith. That's unscriptural for someone who claims to have the gift of healing.

Look at an account of those with the genuine gift of healing in Acts 5:12–16:

> And by the hands of the apostles were many signs and wonders wrought among the people. . . . Insomuch that they brought forth the sick into the streets, and laid them on beds and couches, that at the least the shadow of Peter passing by might overshadow some of them. There came also a multitude out of the cities round about Jerusalem, bringing sick folks, and them which were vexed with unclean spirits: and they were healed every one.

Notice these healings are called "signs." Then those who came to be healed "were healed everyone." Not just some who had enough faith but *everyone.* This is a far cry from what happens in today's healing campaigns by those claiming the gift of healing!

Now, wait a minute, I have no doubt that there have been people healed in some campaigns, but how and why? There are two very valid explanations. One is that every doctor will admit that at least fifty percent of all illnesses are psychosomatic. There is nothing physically wrong with the people; it is all in their minds and it affects them physically. This is a scientifically and medically proven fact. The Christian Scientist's method of "healing" is a good example of proof to any fundamental Bible believer. Many who go to healers are healed in their minds and their physical ailments disappear. Then, secondly, some genuinely born-again people are healed at meetings simply because of their faith and could have been healed at home or in any church if they had exercised such faith beforehand.

One important factor needs to be realized. There is a purpose for illnesses and infirmities and it isn't always God's purpose that everyone be healed. Paul sought God for the thorn in his flesh (whatever it was), but God never healed him and told him that God's "strength was made perfect in weakness." Paul's reply then was, "Most gladly therefore will I rather glory in my infirmities, that the power of Christ may rest upon me" (2 Cor. 12:9). Some need that kind of faith and submission to God today.

Paul was bitten by a serpent and yet not killed (Acts 28:1–6). He healed and cast out evil spirits (Acts 19:11ff.). Paul even raised the dead (Acts 20:9–12). Yet he never healed Timothy but told him to take a little wine for his stomach's sake and infirmities. Take a little medicine (see 1 Tim. 5:23). Why didn't he heal Timothy? It just isn't always God's will to heal. Sometimes sin is in the way and keeps prayers from being answered. There are those who are being chastened (1 Cor. 11:32) and who won't be healed until they confess their sins and faults (James 5:16). As in the case of Paul and Timothy, some infirmities are for the glory of God. Illnesses are not always because of sin, as evidenced by the man born blind, but are so that "the works of God should be made manifest" (John 9:1–3).

God could give the gift of healing today and perhaps does on mission fields to confirm his servants, where the people don't have God's Word in their own language. Yes, I believe in divine healing, and I believe we should preach more on it and pray more for it. Many fundamentalists, I believe, have not been healed because "ye ask not" (James 4:2). The New Testament church ministry of healing is found in James 5. If more would call on the elders to pray and if more elders would pray in faith, much more healing would be seen, but let's not attempt a right thing in a wrong way, as did Saul in 1 Samuel 13:11–14.

It is quite significant that there were a host of so-called big-name faith healers in the 1950s and 1960s. They held big tent campaigns all over the country. Where are they today? Some could not heal anyone, not even themselves, and they died. Why didn't they go to another faith healer and be healed? Some died rather young. Others have just faded out. Still others are in different ministries. What happened to their gift?

These miraculous gifts were used in the early church to confirm the words of those ministering (Mark 16:20). Today we have the Word of God, and our proof of being from God is faithfulness to His Word. When His word is preached, *greater* miracles will be done through the believer in that people will be born of God and healed of sin.

Miracles

John W. Peterson spoke for most of us when he wrote, "I believe in miracles, for I believe in God." If you believe in God, you have to believe in miracles. Someone asked a girl if she believed Jesus had turned the water into wine. She said, "I surely do, for he turned whiskey into milk in our home." Miracles are not hard to believe.

Anyone who has "walked with God" and "poured out his soul" to God in prayer has seen God work miracles in answer to believing prayer. Through eight years of college and seminary, I saw hundreds of miracles of provision and direction in my life and in the lives of fellow students. In thirty years of ministry, miracles have become expected and are of no real surprise at all. In no way could coincidence or happenstance explain all that has happened. Miracles indeed have occurred.

All of this is a far cry, though, from the New Testament "gift of miracles." This "gift of miracles" or "workings of miracles" that the apostles had is quite different from any such claim today. It is my firm belief that this sign gift is no longer in operation in most of the world today. It too was to confirm the word of the early Christians and is no longer needed where the Word of God is published and preached.

The early disciples with this power and authority were to "heal the sick, cleanse the lepers, raise the dead." Where are those who have cleansed the lepers or raised the dead? Again, God could give such gifts today, and perhaps has on mission fields, to serve the same purpose and for the same reasons as in the infant days of the church. When the Word of God is not present in a native language, it can easily parallel apostolic days with the need to confirm God's servants' words with signs and wonders. Reports from mission fields indicate this very well might be the case.

To claim to have this gift in the United States, one certainly would need to prove it just once by raising the dead. It crushes one's heart to see people seeking signs and wonders when they don't care about seeing people born of God. I recall the words of the Lord Jesus: "Rejoice not, that the spirits are subject unto you; but rather rejoice, because your names are written in heaven" (Luke 10:20).

If people who go hundreds of miles and spend thousands of dollars on "miracle meetings" would do all that to get people born of God, we could turn the world upside down once again. Many people are being milked of money and disillusioned by doubt at the emptiness of so many professed miracle workers. When the Lord told them to "heal the sick," He also said in the same verse, "Freely ye have received, freely give" (Matt. 10:8). In love, one could implore those claiming such gifts to "freely give."

Remember, those who boasted of having "done many wonderful works in thy name" were told to "depart . . . I never knew you" (Matt. 7:22,23). Remember also that the Antichrist will come "with all power and signs and lying wonders" (2 Thess. 2:9). No, not everyone professing miracles is of the devil and lost, but there certainly need to be a few more who "try the spirits whether they are of God" (1 John 4:1).

Study Questions: Chapter 13

1. Describe the differences between gifts and talents.
2. What are the differences between gifts and callings?
3. What is the difference between everyone exhorting one another and someone with the gift of exhortation?
4. What are the sign gifts, their role, and their place today?
5. Discuss the gift of prophesying and especially its meaning today.
6. Shouldn't everyone give? What is the gift of giving?

14
How on Earth Are Christians Gifted?

Every Christian is gifted. What a wonderful truth. Have you ever considered yourself gifted? Well, you are if you have a heavenly Father, for God informs us, "Every man hath received a [not *the* in the Greek] gift" (1 Pet. 4:10). Yes, every Christian has received at least one spiritual gift, and it seems, from other Scriptures as well, that everyone has more than one. The average Christian today doesn't consider himself gifted. In fact, the prevalent attitude is to feel terribly inferior and too often even worthless. Every Christian is gifted and needs to live like a gifted person.

Since my childhood I have been impressed with gifted people. Often my mother told me about people who were born "with a silver spoon in their mouths." Neither of my parents had any special talents nor a silver spoon, and my mother often lamented those facts. It was obvious that her son didn't have special talents either. This was all in the human realm, but it left me with feelings of inferiority.

There has been a carryover of this feeling of inferiority into the spiritual realm of my life. As I look back, I realize that one of the main reasons for my feelings of inferiority was that I had not been able to discern what my gifts were. Yes, I knew I had been called of God into Christian service, but I had no idea that my gifts needed to be considered seriously to determine my ministry. It never occurred to me to discover my gifts and use these gifts to their fullest. Oh, I had a wonderful ministry for thirteen years as a pastor. God blessed in unusual ways, but too often the grass would look greener in another field or ministry.

In many ways I wanted to be an evangelist. I loved winning souls, but God never used me in great ways as an evangelist in a public ministry. Sometimes I would see another pastor having a unique ministry, or hear someone tell young preachers that they should build this kind of church or that kind of ministry. Sometimes I'd try their methods. Too often it wasn't successful. I had failed to see that each man has particular gifts to give a special emphasis in his church. Unless one has the same gift, he cannot have the same ministry. This is fundamental and should be in one's conscious consideration as he serves the Lord.

"Who am I?" is the common cry of most people. People are always trying to "find" themselves. Until these matters are settled, a person can wander aimlessly and live a frustrated life. In a real sense, the Christian should know who he is, "a child of God in the service of the King"; but what many are really seeking is their purpose in life. This can be realized fully only when one discovers his gifts.

A 747 jet airplane is a fantastic airplane. Wouldn't it be ridiculous for a pilot to land it in the middle of the Atlantic Ocean and tell all the passengers to get an oar and help row across? The plane wasn't made to float on the ocean but to fly in the sky. When it is used properly, it is beneficial. Many people are helped, and travel is a delight.

So it is with a Christian. What a release from strain and frustration when one finds out what God designed him to do and what gift He has given him to carry out his role in life. No Christian is made to sit, soak, and sour in a church. What an awful waste to let a beautiful Cadillac sit in a garage while the whole household walks. Then, too, how tragic it would be if you took the Cadillac out on a runway, drove it at a hundred miles an hour, and tried to make it fly. It would end up a wreck. That's what happens to many Christians who try to do something God has never gifted them to do. Do you see, then, how important it is to discover your gifts?

First Corinthians 12 gives the most instruction concerning spiritual gifts. In the first verse God starts out by saying, "I don't want you to be ignorant concerning spiritual gifts." Satan surely does, though, and it seems he does a pretty good job. Do you know your gifts?

Verses 3–6 tell us three specific things about gifts. First, there are different gifts. These are named in verses 8–11, and we shall look at them in detail a little later. The important thing to know is that all Christians do not have the same gift. To each his own!

Notice also that gifts are divided "to every man severally as *he will*" (v. 11, italics mine). A Christian must acknowledge the sovereignty of God, or he will never become a stable Christian. There are things that God does that are His business and His alone. Until a Christian *accepts himself* as he is, he will never know peace.

God did not make a mistake when He made you just as you are. He has a great plan and knows just how to get the most out of you, if you are as clay in a potter's hand. You will find complete contentment if you do, and life will be rewarding and fulfilling. It may not always be the easiest road, but in the end it will most certainly be worth it all.

The advertisements that say, "Maybe you should have been a blonde; blondes have more fun," are sheer stupidity. It is an attack on God. The implication is that God made a mistake. He didn't, and Christians must realize and accept that fact. Blind Fanny Crosby would have never given the world hundreds of wonderful hymns had she sat around bemoaning her blindness! God said that He put each of us in the body of Christ "as it hath pleased him" (v. 18). You can trust the Man who made the stars that He did it for our good and His glory and go on from there to see His perfect plan take place in your life.

In verse 13 God gives us the answer as to when we receive our spiritual gifts. It is at the moment of salvation. God declares, "We are all baptized into one body." In chapter 9 we saw that this union to one another in the body of Christ takes place the moment one is saved. To repeat one fact, this baptism by the Holy Spirit into the body of Christ is how one gets "in Christ," and "if any man be in Christ, he is a new creature [creation]" (2 Cor. 5:17). He is saved. This was spoken to the Corinthians, who were carnal Christians (3:1), not super Christians who had attained some high standard of holy living. A Christian's role in the body, whether a finger or a foot, is determined at that moment of salvation. He is then and there equipped with gifts to carry out his functions in the body. He must then discover his gifts so that he can function properly and efficiently.

There is only one body but many members. This is a vital piece of information for you. First Corinthians 12:15 says, "If the foot shall say, Because I am not the hand, I am not of the body; is it therefore not of the body?" Of course, each member is different and has a different function, but all are important parts of the body. Because of this, "The eye cannot say unto the hand, I have no need of thee" (v. 21). In the physical body, no one would think of such a thing, but tragically some members of the body of Christ think such things of one another. These things ought not to be!

Verse 22 brings out the fact that those members which seem to be more feeble are necessary, and indeed they are. Most of us don't have a lot of pride in the looks of our feet. Most of the time they are kept covered but, oh, how we would hate to be without them.

Probably one of the most important lessons about God giving different gifts to each of us is "that there should be no schism [division] in the body" (v. 25). It is a sad story across the land that where the so-called "gift of tongues" has come into churches, it almost consistently brings division. No one doubts for one minute the sincerity of those claiming their gift or of their having had a real experience of "speaking in tongues," but if it is of God, why is there so much division over it? ("Hast thou faith? have it to thyself" [Rom. 14:22].)

Another important factor is brought out in 1 Corinthians 12:29,30: "Are all apostles? are all prophets? are all teachers? are all workers of miracles? Have all the gifts of healing? do all speak with tongues? do all interpret?" The obvious reason for these statements and the conclusion is, no, all do not have the same gifts. Why do some go around trying to get everyone to have the "gift of tongues"? Why not everyone go after the gift of giving? If every Christian had this gift and exercised it, we could buy up every bit of prime time on television and blanket the world with the gospel tomorrow. We could send much-needed ministries around the world. Diversities of tongues is named last, but some put it first on their priority list.

DISCOVER YOUR GIFT

The first thing that ought to be done to discern your gift is to pray. No, it is not trite to say "pray." Don't overlook this. Don't minimize it. "Ye have not, because ye ask not" (James 4:2) does not apply only to obtaining material things but to getting anything from the Lord! "If any of you lack wisdom, let him ask of God" (James 1:5). If you want spiritual wisdom to discern spiritual gifts, then *ask*. If a Christian becomes as serious about asking about his gifts as he is in asking God to give him something he really wants, he will certainly get the answer.

A second way to discern your gift is to notice what you really enjoy doing for the Lord. Ask someone who has the gift of teaching, and he will tell you that he dearly loves to study and prepare and to teach the Word of God. God has given me a gift of exhortation. I dearly love to share a blessing, challenge an audience. and excite others about the Lord. It is a gift, and I love doing it for the glory of the Lord and the good of others.

The idea that "if you don't like to do something, God will make you do it every time" is a terrible misunderstanding about God. God isn't some sadist deliberately calling people to do something or go some place that is obnoxious to them. The contrary is true when we consider Philippians 2:13, "For it is God which worketh in you both to will and to do of his good pleasure." He works within first to will, to desire to do his good pleasure. Those happiest in His service and using their gifts will tell you there is a great desire in their hearts to use the gifts they have.

What seems to come rather naturally or easiest is usually indicative of a gift. Gifts are God-given abilities, and when one finds he has an ability, it seems natural to use that gift.

Those who counsel many young people often find someone trying to serve the Lord in a capacity for which he isn't gifted. The natural advice is this: That just isn't your gift, and you should consider something else. If it is a gift of the Lord, it may need developing, but you should at least find a measure of naturalness in doing it.

The areas in which God obviously uses you can identify a gift. One may sense that God lays it on his heart to give others money from time to time. The recipients may comment how God used him to meet a real need. This could be the beginning of his awareness of the gift of giving.

After my first year of college, I came home and was asked to help work with the young people. They had a Tuesday night Bible study. I felt I knew so terribly little, but I shared with them some things I had learned in my Bible classes. One after another remarked how much he was learning and that I had made it so easy to understand. It made me aware that, to some degree at least, I had a gift or an ability to teach, and so I took every opportunity to develop and exercise that gift.

One good way to discern your gift is to ask others what they think your gifts are. Your pastor especially can discern spiritual gifts in his church members and could help you.

One day I preached in a church in Chicago. The dear Lord blessed, and several decisions were made public. After the service, the chairman of the deacons came to me and blurted out, "Man, you have the gift of exhortation!" And I realized at that time that I did have that gift but had never even thought about it before. Already I had pastored for thirteen years, and yet did not know I had such a gift! This incident is the reason I emphasize so strongly that Christians should discover their gifts. This did worlds of good for me.

The trial-and-error method can work to show what gifts one has. Try teaching a Sunday school class. You might discover a gift of teaching. When help is needed in a church for any occasion, volunteer and see if you seem to fit right in. You may have the gift of helps. We had a man in a church I pastored who just had a knack for being in the right place at the right time to help. Dozens of people were conscious of the times this man had helped them. He was a happy man, and life was rich for him.

DEVELOP YOUR GIFT

The most obvious gift to develop and enhance is the gift of teaching. One who has this gift should study diligently. If he senses a call to Christian ministry, by all means he should go to a Christian school and train to teach. There are methods, techniques, and skills one needs to learn in order to communicate better. Every Christian school—grade school through college—is looking for God-called and well-trained teachers. Always there is a place for those with the gift of teaching to teach Bible, theology, and the many related subjects for the ministry.

Many with a gift of teaching who are not called to "full-time" ministry of teaching are of utmost importance in the local church. Too often people are placed as teachers in Sunday school with no consideration as to their gifts. Some endure it all and struggle through one Sunday after another with a class of boys or girls. Usually there will be a hurried glance through the quarterly late on Saturday night. In the Sunday school class it is easy to fake it with ten- or twelve-year-old boys. The sad thing is that the boys learn nothing, get a soured attitude toward Sunday school, and feel that the Bible isn't interesting. Churches should find those with the gift of teaching and use only them to teach Sunday school, even if several classes have to be combined.

Take the gift of giving. There are probably people whom God would bless unbelievably if they would exercise their gift of giving. I know of several people God has blessed with large amounts of money, because they were faithful in giving and found that they have the gift of giving. The next time the Holy Spirit prompts you to give an extra amount of money to a special cause or in the regular offering of the church, respond and see if God might not have given you the gift of giving. It could open a whole new life for you.

Think about the gift of faith. Begin to claim promises for special needs. Not just your own needs but the needs of your church, of Christian ministries, or your friends. No one should sell all that he has, give it so some ministry, and say, "I'm going to just trust God for everything," unless he has the gift of faith. There are a few people who could live by faith totally, apart from any fixed or known income, but to do so one must have the gift of faith.

DISPENSE YOUR GIFT (USE IT OR LOSE IT)

Just find your gift and exercise it. Hebrews 5:12–14 says:

For when for the time ye ought to be teachers, ye have need that one teach you again which be the first principles of the oracles of God; and are become such as have need of milk, and not of strong meat. For every one that useth milk is unskilful in the word of righteousness: for he is a babe. But strong meat belongeth to them that are of full age, even those who by reason of use have their senses exercised to discern both good and evil

The writer points out that a teacher's senses are exercised "by reason of use" of what God has given. The other side of the coin is that one who doesn't use what has been given loses the use of it and needs to learn *again* the first principles of the oracles of God.

There are two parables given that have great instruction. In Luke 19:11ff. the Lord tells about the nobleman who went away and left a pound with each of his ten servants. A pound was equal to one hundred denarii, or about sixteen dollars in our money. The nobleman told them to "occupy til I come." The word "occupy" here is a business term that meant to "put to trading." "Put it to use," he said, "and make more money for me."

You know the story. When the nobleman returned, one servant came to him and had gained ten pounds. He was rewarded by ruling over ten cities. Another gained five pounds and was duly rewarded. A third brought his pound and felt secure in that he had kept it in a napkin for his master. He was severely reprimanded and the pound was taken away from him, because he had not put it to use. Then God said, "Unto every one which hath shall be given; and from him that hath not, even that he hath shall be taken away from him" (Luke 19:26). What did he mean? He meant, "To him who has put to use what God gave him shall be given more. He who has not put to use what was given him, even that shall be taken away from him."

God does say, "The gifts and calling of God are without repentance" (Rom. 11:29), but when a Christian doesn't put to use what God gives him, he will lose it all when he stands before God. It also seems that the Christian who doesn't put to use what the Lord has given him will sooner or later lose the use of that now. Many Christians who wasted their lives in their younger days seem to have no ability at all for God in their later years. Might it be that God has taken away that which they had? It's an awesome responsibility to be endowed by the Lord of glory and then not be a good steward. Christians must discover their gifts and put them to use in the kingdom of God.

In one sense, everyone is given an equal amount by God. Each servant had one pound. Each of us can look around and find others with far more abilities, but in a sense each has equal opportunity and can increase his "earnings" tenfold as the one servant did. This can be a great encouragement to each person.

Then in Matthew 25:14ff. each servant is given a different amount. One is given five talents, another two, and another one talent. A talent was about $960 in our money. The one with five gained five more, the one with two gained two, but the servant with one talent had hid it and gained nothing. He too was severely reprimanded, and again it was said, "From him that hath not shall be taken away even that which he hath" (v. 29). It's so important to see that Christians must put to use all the gifts God gives them. No one can hide his light under a bushel.

Note that the one with two talents was rewarded the same as the one with five, for both had gained an amount equal to that which they had. This should encourage each person, even though he finds others with far more gifts or abilities. He can have the same reward as the one with many more gifts. How wonderful! How fair and honorable is God in all His dealing.

Another revealing truth is that it was the man with only one talent who didn't put it to use. Now, there is a mystery that I don't believe can really be solved here. In practical living today, when someone really begins to serve the Lord and put to use what God has given him, it seems that he discovers new gifts and abilities. The question is, Does God give more gifts when someone uses what he has given him? Or does he already have the gifts but only discovers them when the known gifts are used? It doesn't really matter which is true; the important thing is to be faithful with what one has and knows.

There are a couple of important admonitions concerning gifts that should be carefully heeded. Paul warned Timothy, "Neglect not the gift that is in thee" (1 Tim. 4:14). To obey this admonition one surely needs to know his gifts. All Christians are affected when a person neglects his gift. It was given to be used, and it won't wear out!

Timothy was also exhorted to "stir up the gift of God, which is in thee" (2 Tim. 1:6). In Hebrews 5:14 we are exercised to discern both good and evil "by reason of use." So one's gifts are stirred up "by reason of use," even as one's muscles are. A Christian must not let his gifts lie dormant. How terribly wasteful that so few Christians have even discovered their gifts and that only a small percentage of them actively use them. The whole body of Christ needs to be stretched and exercised into action.

Study Questions: Chapter 14

1. Is every Christian gifted? Why? What effect should it have on each believer?
2. How does one discover his gifts?
3. What does it mean, "to him that hath shall be given"?
4. What should be a Christian's attitude concerning the fact that some have more gifts than others?
5. What were Paul's admonitions to Timothy concerning gifts, and how do his words apply to us today?

15
What on Earth
Is God's Will?

Why am I here? Where am I headed? These two questions plague many people throughout their lives. Without a purpose, life is meaningless. Life is like a ship without a rudder unless one has real reason for existing. Man is basically a goal-getter. A person will not be a go-getter until he has a goal. Someone has said that behind every successful man is a devoted wife and a surprised mother-in-law. This may be true, but it is more true that in front of every successful man is a goal and a purpose that motivate him.

The great God who made us also gave us a plan and a purpose for life as well. There is a "good, and acceptable, and perfect, will of God" (Rom. 12:2) for each child of God. The tragedy of life is not what men suffer, but what they miss. To miss the will of God is like missing a turn and being lost on a highway or getting on a long detour and losing hours of time on a bumpy road. Life is bumpy enough without getting on the wrong road.

God did not promise "skies always blue." In fact, He promised, "In the world ye shall have tribulation" (John 16:33). Knowing you are on the right road, in the race, and headed toward the goal will sustain you when others fall behind and drop out.

The apostle Paul was a good example of this truth. Paul was at Miletus, giving a farewell to the elders of Ephesus. He concluded his farewell by saying:

> And now, behold, I go bound in the spirit unto Jerusalem, not knowing the things that shall befall me there: Save that the Holy Ghost witnesseth in every city, saying that bonds and afflictions abide me. But none of these things move me, neither count I my life dear unto myself, so that I might finish my course with joy, and the ministry, which I have

received of the Lord Jesus, to testify the gospel of the grace of God (Acts 20:22–24).

Paul, who knew what it was to be beaten and imprisoned, knew that more of the same awaited him as he headed toward Jerusalem. But with a note of victory and joy, he said, "None of these things move me." They didn't bother him at all. He was not disturbed and would not be deterred, for he wanted to "finish my course." He was in the race all the way. He knew God's purpose and plan for his life, and he pressed on. What a thrill of fulfillment he must have had all through life. He could and did take anything life held out to him, not with a doleful or defeatist manner, but with a victorious and joyful attitude.

As Paul was about to cross the finish line, he triumphantly said, "I have fought a good fight, I have finished my course, I have kept the faith: Henceforth there is laid up for me a crown of righteousness, which the Lord, the righteous judge, shall give me at that day: and not to me only, but unto all them also that love his appearing" (2 Tim. 4:7,8). Every Christian needs to find the will of God for his own life, to run the race, and to finish the course with the same feeling of accomplishment.

The idea of course is rather like an obstacle course or a race track. God has a course and direction for each life. How is your track record these days? Have you found your course? Are you in the race? Are you running well? Are you tiring in the race? Are you about to quit before the finish? Hang in there. It will be worth it all when we see Jesus!

FALSE FEELINGS ABOUT THE WILL OF GOD

Satan always tries to fake us out. He clouds the issue all the time. He directs us down a dead-end road or up a blind alley. There are many false feelings about the will of God.

One false feeling is that the will of God is unpleasant. How often someone has said, "I just know if I surrender my life to the Lord, He is going to call me to be a missionary to the jagged jungles of Brazil, or to the hottest heart of Africa, or to the poverty parts of India." Many live with the attitude that God is just waiting to give Christians the most deprived existence possible as soon as He has control of their lives. A lot of people think of the will of God in terms of, "You can't do this," and "You mustn't go there," and "No more of that." These are just some of the deceits of the devil. God gives His best to those who leave the choice to Him. The truth is that the will of God is *good* (Rom. 12:2). Just a little logic would dispel any deceit.

Suppose your son, with whom you always have a hassle about cleaning his room or taking out the garbage, were to announce to you, "Dad, I've been wrong to disobey you. From now on you won't have to ask me twice. Whatever you tell me to do, I'm going to do it from my heart right away." You say, "I'd faint." Yes, probably, but would you then say, "I've been waiting for this. Wash the car; rake the yard. I'm going to make life miserable for you." No, a thousand times no! Why, you would probably hug him, and then take him out for the biggest steak dinner and ice cream soda that he had ever seen. How can one attribute to sinful man a better attitude and response to his son than God would have to one of His own children? God Himself made just the opposite comparison when He said, "If ye then, being evil, know how to give good gifts unto your children, how much more shall your Father which is in heaven give good things to them that ask him?" (Matt. 7:11). God is *good,* and His will is good and perfect! Don't stay away from God because of such false feelings.

A second false feeling is that the will of God is hard to find. If thoughts were bared, a host of people would be found to feel that God plays cat and mouse with them concerning His will. Some people feel like the mule with the carrot hung just out of his reach to keep him going. Others think the will of God is some kind of mysterious puzzle with a gimmick they have to hunt for.

The truth is that one of the primary purposes God saved

us was to show us His will for our lives. He indicated this in Acts 22:14 when He said to Paul, "The God of our fathers hath chosen thee, that thou shouldest know his will." Isn't that fantastic? God chose you that you should know His will. He *wants* to show His will. In fact, He is far more anxious for us to know His will than we are to find it. No, it's not hard to find if one really wants to know it.

Another promise that could fit so well here is John 7:17: "If any man will do his will, he shall know of the doctrine, whether it be of God, or whether I speak of myself." A simple translation here would be, "If any man wants to do His will," God says he shall know whether it is a doctrine or a deed. Again, Christians need to repent of false concepts, and in faith trust God and believe Him to find His will. No doubt some haven't found the will of God because of violating the principle of the double-minded man of James 1:5–8 who indeed shall not receive anything of the Lord.

A third false feeling is that the will of God is for professionals only; that is, that God has His will for those in "full-time Christian service," but others just knock about on their own. This is obviously false, for in the body of Christ, "God set the members every one of them in the body, as it hath pleased him" (1 Cor. 12:18). How wonderful that everyone is included in the will of God, and that He designed each one as it pleased Himself! Yes, and all are necessary (v. 22). God speaks of rulers as the ministers of God (Rom. 13:4). Just as there is a specific purpose and function for our hands, so God has a purpose and function for each member of His body, no matter how insignificant any member might deem himself.

A fourth false feeling is that the will of God involves only the big things of life. How sad to be robbed by this false feeling. Remember how the dear Lord told of His personal awareness of the common and small sparrow (Matt. 10:29). Imagine that the very hairs on our heads are numbered (Matt. 10:30). And, of course, He was very much aware of the unknown widow and her two mites. Yes, God is vitally aware of the minute things of our lives.

Recently I was with a fairly new Christian. We pulled up in front of a busy store and found a car pulling out just in front of us, leaving a parking place. He called me lucky. I told him that I had just prayed for a parking place a minute before. He was surprised to find it natural and right to pray about even a parking place. It's a wonderful way to live, knowing that God is interested in such small things and that we can pray about them.

It's wrong to be concerned about the unknown and ignore or neglect the known. Some people who are always trying to "find the will of God" are doing very little about the revealed will of God. It is good to find the will of God and to know the will of God, but it is best to be in the will of God and to do the will of God day by day. If one stays in fellowship with the Lord and lives in the will of God as he knows it day by day, he is bound to "find" the "will of God" as he comes to it in the future.

God doesn't always reveal His will for us very far in advance. Sometimes it would scare us. Often we aren't ready for it. Many who have been serving God for any length of time can look back and thank God that He didn't tell them twenty or thirty years before what they would be doing at the present time.

God put me through nine years of college and seminary, fourteen years of pastoring, and twelve years of educational ministry to prepare me for my present position. All of my experiences were necessary to qualify me to do what I do now. As a younger Christian, too often I became more concerned about the years ahead than the opportunities of the present. Now, I know that if we are faithful and obedient to what we know we are to do, He will show us the next step. The principles of the verse, "Unto every one that hath shall be given" (Matt. 25:29), applies aptly here as well. God is saying to him who has done His will *now* that he will receive even more knowledge of His will. Someone has said, "What I don't know about the will of God doesn't disturb me; it's what I do know that disturbs me, knowing I'm going to have to give an account for it all." Someone else has said,

"What I know about God and His will leads me to trust Him implicitly for what I don't know!"

The known will of God is challenging and demanding. It should occupy our time and efforts to the utmost. Being involved to fulfil the known will of God will surely make Romans 12:21 a reality: "Be not overcome of evil, but overcome evil with good."

WHAT IS THE WILL OF GOD?

One thing for sure is that God is "not willing that any should perish, but that all should come to repentance" (2 Pet. 3:9). Again, Paul declares God's will by saying that He "will have all men to be saved" (1 Tim. 2:4). Christians are to get the gospel "to every creature" (Mark 16:15). "Ye shall be witnesses unto me" (Acts 1:8) is for every believer. This should not be a drudgery or a fearsome thing to Christians.

If someone's employer gave him a job to do and that person didn't know how to accomplish the task, he would go to the proper person and find out how to do it. Rather than sit and do nothing, live in fear about it, lie, and give excuses for disobedience, Christians should go to pastors, get the proper instructions and training, and get on with the job. What if Noah had said, "God, I never built an ark before. I'm afraid of what people will say. I just don't feel cut out to be a shipbuilder." The consequences are obvious. So should it be concerning this known will of God to witness.

As I write at this moment, I am on a plane from Amman, Jordan. The past two days a group of us were in Amman on a tour through the Bible lands, and we went shopping on New Year's Day. An English-speaking Jordanian named Hamada spoke to us and offered to help us by interpreting with shopkeepers. As we walked along, I began to share the gospel with him. He was a Muslim. When I told him that God loved him, and how Christ died for him, he was shocked and said, "I never knew that, nor heard it before." His heart was greatly prepared by God, and right there on the street, amid a throng of people passing by, he prayed out loud and invited the Lord Jesus into his heart to be his Savior. I invited him to our hotel that evening to talk further. He came and brought a friend. His friend spoke very little English, but with Hamada interpreting, he too received Christ.

At the hotel I asked the desk clerk if there was a Baptist church in town. He said he knew a Baptist minister personally, and even knew his phone number! The minister had been witnessing to him over a period of weeks. We called the minister. In the providence of the great God we serve, he, David Wilson, was a graduate of Moody Bible Institute where I used to teach! Of course, he came immediately to the hotel. David Wilson spent two hours with them, talking in their native language. David, who knows the real issues in dealing with Muslims, felt Hamada had really trusted Christ. Another meeting was scheduled for the following night at David's house for discipling. Hamada came, and this time brought two more friends! GLORY!

Now, I didn't have to pray and fast or have some special feeling to know God's will to witness to Hamada when we met on the street. We were told two thousand years ago to get the gospel to every creature. It is simply a matter of doing it graciously in the power of the Spirit.

What is the will of God? "In every thing give thanks: for this is the will of God in Christ Jesus concerning you" (1 Thess. 5:18). This is a revolutionary principle to live by. The natural tendency is to complain or fret or be anxious, when all the time "all things work together for good to them that love God" (Rom. 8:28). Since this is true, the Christian can give thanks *in everything*. No matter what occurs or what the circumstances, I can be sure it is all for my good, and I ought to be thankful. Complaining or fretting is simply not believing that God is allowing everything for my good.

Several years ago the dear Lord was trying to teach me the wonders of this truth. One day I had a slight automobile accident, and it was my fault. When it happened I immediately checked and saw that the two people with me were not hurt, and the Holy Spirit reminded me to give thanks, which I did. I took the car to a shop for an eight-hundred-dollar repair job. As the manager and I concluded our business, I shared the gospel with him and asked if he would receive the Lord Jesus Christ. He blurted out, "I think it's time I did." Bless the Lord, the manager, Max, prayed out loud to receive the Savior. In a few minutes my wife came in. I introduced them and asked if he could tell my wife what he had just done. He turned to her and said, "Well, he got me; I just got saved." If that were the end of the story, it would be wonderful enough.

A week later I dropped in to see how he was doing. He kept saying, "You won't believe what has been happening." He told of another victory over habits and attitudes in his life. As we were talking, another man came up. Max had to go into an office to get something for the man, and he said to me, "Preacher, tell him what you told me last week." I did, and when I finished presenting the gospel, I asked if he wouldn't like to receive Christ. He replied exactly as Max had a week before in the same spot: "I think it's time I did." He too prayed out loud and accepted Christ. Presently, Max returned, and his friend blurted out to Max, "Well, he got another one!" I felt as if I were seeing a rerun, so much was exactly as it had been a week before.

What if I had gotten all hot and bothered about the accident and had not given thanks? Frankly, I believe I would have missed the whole experience. Yes, in *everything* give thanks. There should be no place for murmuring and complaining in the Christian life.

"For this is the will of God, even your sanctification, that ye should abstain from fornication" (1 Thess. 4:3). This fact should go without saying, but even as in Paul's day the admonition is needed today. A permissive society and worldly mores cannot set the standards of conduct. The best way to live in the world is to live above it. No matter how much name-calling and ridicule one must take, it is still the will of God to abstain from fornication.

The most important stated will of God for the Christian is to be filled with the Holy Spirit. Paul puts it this way,

"Wherefore, be ye not unwise, but understanding what the will of the Lord is. And be not drunk with wine, wherein is excess; but be filled with the Spirit" (Eph. 5:17,18). This should be of great encouragement to every believer, for it declares that there is no question but that it is the will of God for every believer to have the control and power of the Holy Spirit. No Christian needs to be fruitless or powerless. God wants every Christian to experience the fullness of His Holy Spirit. No need to feel left out. No need to wonder if God wants you to know this Spirit-filled life. The answer is an emphatic *yes*. Are you appropriating all of this in your life by exercising faith in the promise of God?

HOW DO YOU FIND THE WILL OF GOD?

There seems to be a pattern for finding the will of God for Christian service and answering the call of God. In the Word of God are three steps that most people have experienced as they were called into Christian service.

1. Dedication

The first step is illustrated in the call of Samuel. God called Samuel, and Samuel thought it was Eli the priest calling. He ran to Eli and said, "Here am I; for thou didst call me" (1 Sam. 3:6). The Bible said Eli's eyes had grown dim (v. 2), but his spiritual sight was dimmer and he didn't realize it was God until God called Samuel the third time. Many today seem not to discern God calling young people, and just tell them to go lie down, as Eli did to Samuel. Finally, Eli realized what was happening and told Samuel to answer the Lord the next time by saying, "Speak, Lord, for thy servant heareth" (v. 9).

This step I believe is *dedication*. Many feel an inner tug at their heart. A lot of young people have a yearning and desire to do something for God but do not know for sure whether it is the call of God. The answer to them should be the same as to Samuel: "Speak, Lord, for thy servant heareth." This implies dedication, for he is to call Him *Lord*. Then he is to say, "I'm listening and willing. I want to know what you want me to do." The cry of his heart should be Paul's prayer: "Lord, what wilt thou have me to do?" (Acts 9:6). Most of us remember the day when we dedicated our lives to the Lord. The secret to an unsatisfied life often lies in an unsurrendered will.

2. Determination

The next step that the dear Lord requires is what Isaiah experienced when he was shown the high and holy God (Isa. 6:1–3). By seeing God exalted he saw his own sinfulness and that of those around him (v. 5). He began to see people lost and without God. Then God asked, "Whom shall I send, and who will go for us?" (v. 8). With his heart touched by God, Isaiah replied, "Here am I; send me" (v. 8). This whole scene is familiar to anyone who has known the call of God in his life. As he sees a sinful world going to hell and his own heart moved by God, all else seems so unimportant and shallow next to getting the gospel to every living creature. This step is *determination* based on desire.

This desire seems to be the key to the call of God. In Philippians 2:13 we are informed, "It is God which worketh in you both to will and to do of his good pleasure." The word for "will" here comes from the Greek word *Thelo* which means "to will or want to or desire." The question is, "Where does anyone get a desire to do anything for God?" The answer is, "It comes from God." This is the call of God. The world certainly would not give anyone a desire to do God's good pleasure. Surely Satan wouldn't either. And of course, the flesh doesn't want to please God.

So the only conclusion is that if a person has a desire, a hunger, a longing to do anything for God, he can be sure God put it there. Any Christian would acknowledge that God has to work in him to *do* God's good pleasure, but what is overlooked is that God gives him even *the desire* to do His good pleasure. This, I submit, is the call of God to preach or teach or reach people for Christ in any ministry whatsoever. If someone wants to preach because he feels it is a prestigious position or for any other reason, that is not a call of God. If, on the other hand, someone has a burning desire to do God's good pleasure by preaching the gospel to every creature, he can answer, "Here am I, send me," with the confidence that God has called.

3. Destination

The only question then is *where*. Where does God want you to serve? When Paul and others planned to go to Bithynia, "the Spirit suffered them not," and they received the famed Macedonian call which said, "Come over into Macedonia, and help us" (Acts 16:9). When one is heading in the direction he knows to go, God can always steer him to the exact destination He wants. Often I have seen God do this very thing. He will close one door and then obviously open another. When the open door is entered, it becomes obvious that God has led him to the very spot He wants him. Christians must not fall prey to the temptation not to move until they see the end of the road and have all the answers. Like a game of checkers, it is usually one move at a time until arriving at the *destination* God has planned.

All this gives the answer for the will of God concerning a call to service. What about the will of God in everyday decisions and directions? Here are eight positive procedures to find the will of God:

1. *Prayer.* Immediately when Paul met Christ, he prayed, "Lord, what wilt thou have me to do?" (Acts 9:6). This would make an excellent daily prayer for one seeking the will of God for his life. (May I suggest typing or printing it on a card and taping it to your mirror to remind you to pray about this often?) "You have not because you ask not" can also apply to not having a knowledge of God's will for one's life.

2. *Word.* The psalmist said, "Thy word is a lamp unto my feet, and a light unto my path" (Ps. 119:105). The Holy Spirit uses the Word to give us direction. You will never know the will of God if you neglect the Word of God. An often futile method of using the Bible for direction is to open it at random and, without looking, plant your finger on a verse and expect God to have His directions revealed in the verse.

3. *Counsel.* "In the multitude of counsellors there is safety" (Prov. 11:14). God sent Cornelius to Peter for wisdom. Scores of young people have found God's will through counseling with a mature Christian.

4. *Sermon.* "And the two disciples heard him [John the Baptist] speak, and they followed Jesus" (John 1:37). Often God calls men to preach through a sermon.

5. *Parents.* "Children, obey your parents in all things: for this is well pleasing unto the Lord" (Col. 3:20). In God's chain of command, God often shows His will for an individual as he follows the instructions of a parent. Even the Lord Jesus was subject to His earthly parents (Luke 2:51).

6. *Circumstances.* If "all things work together for good to them that love God" (Rom. 8:28), then the Christian can be sure the circumstances that befall him are ordained of God and often contain the direction of the Lord. The selling of Joseph to the Ishmaelites in Genesis 37:27 would seem like a travesty without knowing the end of the story where we see the direction of God demonstrated in an unusual way.

7. *Abilities.* One of the most obvious ways to find God's direction is to discover God's gift or gifts that you possess. The Bible tells how "all Israel from Dan even to Beersheba knew that Samuel was established to be a prophet of the Lord" (1 Sam. 3:20). You and others will be able to discern what God has for you as you discern what He has gifted you to do.

8. *The Holy Spirit.* As the Spirit stopped Paul from going to Bithynia and then opened the door to Macedonia, so He will guide you as you walk in the Spirit (Gal. 5:16) and are led by the Spirit (Rom. 8:14).

A final test of the will of God for one walking in the Spirit is to "let the peace of God rule in your hearts" (Col. 3:15). The word for *rule* here means "to judge, arbitrate, or umpire." If one is led by the Spirit he will have "the fruit of the Spirit . . . peace" (Gal. 5:22). This is a delicate situation and can be discerned only by one "filled with the Spirit" (Eph. 5:18), but it is the one criterion God has declared to be the "umpire" in our lives. A good rule is, "If it's doubtful, don't." First John 3:21 says, "Beloved, if our heart condemn us not, then have we confidence toward God." If it's the will of God, you will have the peace of God in your heart. My wife and I for twenty-eight years have found this to be a great guide to the will of God. God has given us both perfect peace about every decision we have made. If one of us lacked peace, we prayed about the matter until He either changed our minds and directions or in His time gave us the peace, and we knew His will.

In closing, consider these seven statements and injunctions:

1. Be willing to do whatsoever He might show you.
2. Be filling your mind with the Word of God.
3. Be thrilling your soul in prayer and fellowship with the Lord.
4. God's calling is simply understanding God's will for your life.
5. Always be satisfied with the next step and don't worry about the whole plan.
6. If uncertain of the next step, keep on doing what you're doing until He shows you differently.
7. Don't let your desire to know God's will become an anxiety to you.

Remember, "If we do God's will as we know it, we shall know God's will to do it." Where the Good Shepherd guides, He provides. God gives His best to those who leave the choice to Him.

Study Questions: Chapter 15

1. Does God have a purpose for every life? Discuss it.
2. What are some common false feelings about the will of God?

3. What are some things stated to be the will of God for every believer?
4. How does one find the will of God for himself?
5. What are the eight procedures given for finding the will of God?

16
Why on Earth
Should I Fast?

"Moreover when ye fast . . ." (Matt. 6:16). When did you last fast? The attitude seems to be that to talk about fasting just isn't done. Some people almost make you feel as if you belong to a cult if you fast. For too long, fasting has been looked upon as belonging to some extremist group. Some Christians feel that they know better than to do it or don't need it.

Notice in Matthew 6 that Jesus talked about fasting in almost the same breath that He talked about praying and giving. In verses 1–4 He talks about giving and the right and wrong way to do it. In verses 5–15 much is said about prayer. Then, in verses 16–18, in the most natural way, He begins talking about fasting. He didn't say, "If you fast," but "When you fast." There was no question but that the disciples would fast, just as they would pray. Fasting is a vital spiritual exercise, as is prayer. The majority of fundamental Christians haven't looked upon it in that manner. Some twenty years ago I preached a message instructing our people on the joy and the way of fasting. The next word came to me that people were saying I wasn't a Baptist because I preached on fasting. Today much more is being said and preached and even practiced concerning fasting.

Jesus certainly fasted. He fasted for forty days and forty nights on the occasion before He was tempted of Satan (Matt. 4:2). In Acts 13 the church at Antioch fasted and prayed. While they were engaged in these spiritual exercises, God called Barnabas and Saul. Now, that was quite a fruitful result. No doubt more servants of God would be called from churches if they engaged more in fasting than in feasting. The church prayed and fasted again when they commissioned the first missionaries. And Paul, too, said he was "in fastings

181

often" (2 Cor. 11:27). Fasting wasn't unfamiliar nor rare to Paul.

"Then came to him the disciples of John, saying, Why do we and the Pharisees fast oft, but thy disciples fast not? And Jesus said unto them, Can the children of the bride-chamber mourn, as long as the bridegroom is with them? but the days will come, when the bridegroom shall be taken from them, and then shall they fast" (Matt. 9:14,15). Without hesitation the Lord Jesus said His disciples would fast when He was taken from them, and so they did, and so should we today. Fasting is for today. Many are learning afresh the joy and spiritual profit of fasting. Could this be a spiritual practice you have neglected and need today? If could be used of God to unlock some wonderful blessings and treasures in your life.

THE POSSIBILITIES OF FASTING

Consider some of the possibilities of fasting as it was practiced by God's people. David fasted as he mourned and wept for Saul and Jonathan. "And they mourned, and wept, and fasted until even, for Saul, and for Jonathan his son, and for the people of the Lord, and for the house of Israel; because they were fallen by the sword" (2 Sam. 1:12). This was a common practice among the children of Israel. Fasting was not done simply because they forgot to eat or were so burdened, but as a spiritual exercise. This seems quite clear in 2 Samuel 12:16 and 21, where it tells about David fasting when his son by Bathsheba was mortally ill. After the child died, "David arose from the earth, and washed, and anointed himself, and changed his apparel, and came into the house of the Lord, and worshipped: for he came to his own house; and when he required, they set bread before him, and he did eat" (v. 20). His servants were perplexed and inquired concerning David's behavior. "And he said, While the child was yet alive, I fasted and wept: for I said, Who can tell whether God will be gracious to me, that the child may live?" (v. 21). Fasting is a vital spiritual exercise and should be practiced today.

Fasting is used to humble one's soul before God. A powerful passage tells about this: "False witnesses did rise up; they laid to my charge things that I knew not. They rewarded me evil for good to the spoiling of my soul. But as for me, when they were sick, my clothing was sackcloth: I humbled my soul with fasting; and my prayer returned into mine own bosom" (Ps. 35:11–13). Everyone has at some time been falsely accused and hurt. No one goes without mistreatment. The difference between the winner and the loser is the response. To retaliate in like kind is to poison one's soul and to become bitter. The psalmist rather "humbled my soul with fasting." Surely all flesh seeks revenge, and fasting is one provision of God for conquering the flesh. Instead of a haughty, vengeful flesh, one can have a humbled victorious flesh through fasting. This could be the formula for victory for many Christians if they would practice this scriptural exercise.

The psalmist David gives another insight into fasting which is extremely profitable. "When I wept, and chastened my soul with fasting" (Ps. 69:10). The word *chastened* is not in the Hebrew text, but nothing better could be placed here in the light of the whole context. To discipline oneself and chasten one's own soul is the dire need of every believer. Nothing could be more profitable, especially when one senses himself cooling off or calming down from the joy of that first love. Too many have fallen to the same low as Israel, whose soul loathed the manna God sent (see Num. 11:6). Their souls need this wonderful provision of God for chastening until they are turned back to God.

Fasting is connected with seeking the Lord. Daniel said, "And I prayed unto the Lord my God, and made my confession, . . . to seek by prayer and supplications, with fasting, and sackcloth, and ashes" (Dan. 9:3,4). This is probably the most common purpose of Christians fasting today. Most who do fast can testify that when there is a hunger in their soul to seek the Lord afresh and more deeply, fasting is a logical exercise and most conducive toward doing it. This has helped many a Christian who once knew a deep desire for God to have that desire restored by seeking the Lord through fasting.

From God's standpoint, He tells His people to turn to Him through fasting. "Therefore also now, saith the Lord, turn ye even to me with all your heart, and with fasting, and with weeping, and with mourning" (Joel 2:12). How often we exhort people to turn to the Lord by every means under the sun except fasting. This element of worship and spiritual exercise is almost nonexistent among the rank and file of God's people. History, ancient and modern, bears testimony to fasting connected with times of turning to God. Great revivals have been preceded by fasting, a vital part of the practice of God's people. It could be a key to God's people turning to God afresh today.

Many other passages give light to fasting, but one beautiful passage gives an insight into fasting which is almost totally overlooked today. About the godly widow Anna it is said, "And she was a widow of about fourscore and four years, which departed not from the temple, but served God with fastings and prayers night and day" (Luke 2:37). This is an outstanding statement. It says she "served God with fastings." Every Christian can't serve God overseas as a missionary, or in the pulpit as a pastor, or on a faculty as a teacher, but all can serve God through fasting. How beautifully one serves God through this denial of the flesh. Doesn't it seem tragic that so few have been instructed in this sacred act of worship and service?

THE PURPOSE OF FASTING

This leads to the purpose of fasting. A simple summary as to its purpose might help us to focus clearly on fasting. First of all, fasting is to deny the flesh. There is a theological use of the word "flesh," but it is closely related to the physical flesh. Bound up in and to the physical flesh is this sinful flesh and its sinful nature. Notice the climax to the indictment of the enemies of the cross in Philippians 3:17–19. "Brethren, be followers together of me, and mark them who walk so as ye have us for an [example]. (For many walk, of whom I have told you often, and now tell you even weeping, that they are the enemies of the cross of Christ: whose end is destruction, whose God is their belly, and whose glory is in their shame, who mind earthly things.)" "Whose God is their belly" could almost be written across America as "Ichabod" was across Israel. We feast when we ought to fast. "Eat, drink, and be merry" is the philosophy and motto of multitudes. Whatever else it does, fasting denies the flesh the fulfillment of its appetites. Strange, isn't it, how the belly howls and growls when it is denied even for a few minutes past the mealtime. Christians who practice fasting find it a great delight to deny the flesh to the glory of God.

A second purpose is to defeat the devil. Whatever might be the connection and the purpose, the Lord Jesus Himself fasted before He faced the temptation of Satan. "Then was Jesus led up of the spirit into the wilderness to be tempted of the devil. And when he had fasted forty days and forty nights, he was afterward an hungred" (Matt. 4:1,2). Then Satan came with all the cunning he could muster, but the victory is well known; he was defeated, and our Savior remained the spotless Lamb of God. Whatever resources of power or reserve of strength may come from fasting, we all need a double dose today. Someone said Paul feared men so little because he feared God so much. Christians would do well to stock up, not with more food from the store, but with more fuel from fasting. Those who have been there can testify of fresh victories. Habits have been broken, new priorities established, and greater goals for living have come through fasting.

This leads to a third purpose of fasting, and that is to deepen spiritual desires. From several passages already cited, this certainly is one result. Somehow, as the flesh is denied, the spirit is stirred. A fresh appetite for the Word of God and prayer is almost an immediate result. Just as smoking, we are told, destroys one's tastebuds, so feasting can destroy spiritual desires and tastebuds. Fasting can arouse spiritual desires and increase them to a new level.

Fasting defies the world as well. Peer pressure on young people is frightening, but the conforming pressure of the world that says, "Don't be different," is terrifying. Nothing seems to baffle the unsaved mind like a fasting Christian. The world just isn't cut out for that. Every Christian has felt the urge to be able to give the devil a swift kick in the seat of the pants. And the Christian can give this old world a slap in the face by saying, "You will not make me conform to you."

Last, one of the highest purposes of fasting is to delight God. God promises to "reward thee openly" (Matt. 6:18), if fasting is carried out correctly. How it must please the heart of God when the heart of man seeks more of the Father in heaven and less of the food of earth.

THE PERFORMANCE OF FASTING

The performance of fasting is simple. It has no mystery. How do you fast? First of all, you do it as unto the Lord. In Christ's day the hypocrites made a big show of this act of worship even as they did of giving and praying. The praise of men was their only fruit or reward. You can fast and go right on with your day's work or ministry. I've taught my classes and been out witnessing or in the hospital visiting, and no one knew a thing about my fasting that day. Jesus said, "When thou fastest, anoint thine head, and wash thy face; that thou appear not unto men to fast" (Matt. 6:17). You can spend the day fasting and simply spend the extra time in prayer during lunch or coffee breaks. A person will find as he fasts that throughout the day there will be an extra consciousness of praying. Of course, you will have whole days set aside to pray, read the Word, and fast. During these days you will have a growing burden of prayer as the day progresses.

The question arises about drinking any liquids. For one day of fasting, usually no juices or foods of any kind are consumed. Most people do not have a problem for just one day. If someone does feel nauseated, he should drink a little juice. Some have a problem going a whole day without anything in their stomachs and even get sick headaches the first time they try it. It seems that if one has a great deal of physical problems as he fasts, so that his mind is just on the fast and he is not enjoying fellowship with the Lord and prayer, then something should be done to eliminate the condition. The first fast isn't always easy. This should not discourage people from trying at another time. Few people can set out to pray for any length of time without having their minds wander and their prayers interrupted. Satan fights prayer, and we may be sure he will fight fasting as well.

How long and how often should you fast? By all means on the first occasion don't plan to fast a week or even several days. Try it for one day, and enjoy the victory of that experience. How often one fasts depends on the need and burden to fast. Some fast one day a week regularly. Some plan on a day a month. There is no set pattern or instruction as to how often. Usually it is done as the burden or need arises. In Zechariah 7:5 and 8:19 it seems clear that they had regularly planned fasts. The Pharisee in Luke 18:12 said he fasted twice a week. Over and over in the Old Testament they "called" a fast or "proclaimed" a fast (2 Chron. 20:3; Joel 1:14; 2:15; Jonah 3:5).

You can see they proclaimed a fast throughout all Judah in 2 Chronicles 20:3. A pastor can call for a day of prayer and fasting in his church. Every time I have done this as a pastor we saw unusual results. We usually had it on a Wednesday and closed out with midweek prayer meeting. I would ask the people not to tell me whether or not they were fasting. We would have a special prayer meeting at the church around ten in the morning for those who could come. Some would stay through lunchtime. Sometimes we would break up at noon for the wives who had lunches to prepare or children coming home. An afternoon prayer meeting might be called to be closed out with the evening prayer meeting. Usually a fast would begin in the morning and go to the next morning. That's where the word "breakfast" comes from—it means to "break a fast." There have been times when I fasted only one or two meals in a day because of circumstances.

Fasting is scriptural. Fasting is a spiritual exercise even as praying is. If you have never engaged in this spiritual experience, you should try it. It can be a blessed day.

Study Questions: Chapter 16

1. What other spiritual exercises are discussed in the same Scripture passage that discusses fasting?
2. List some reasons why we know God expects Christians to fast.
3. What are some possibilities for fasting as discussed in this chapter?
4. What are some purposes of fasting?
5. Discuss the practice of fasting.

17
How on Earth Can I Have The Power of God?

There is a power failure in the church today. There is an energy crisis. It is not just a "brownout," but a real lack of power in individual lives and in the average church. The average church makes no impact on peoples' lives. Communities are unaffected by the church. There is no conviction of sin and no conversion of sinners. We are in trouble.

Power is promised and provided: "But ye shall receive power, after that the Holy Ghost is come upon you" (Acts 1:8). This power was promised and given to the early church. They had power to heal. Peter said, "Silver and gold have I none; but such as I have give I thee: In the name of Jesus Christ of Nazareth rise up and walk" (Acts 3:6). The man did rise up and walk. The disciples had no money, but they had power. Today we have the money but no power. Their rulers asked, "By what power . . . have ye done this?" (Acts 4:7). Peter said that power was in Jesus' name (Acts 4:10). So it is today.

The disciples had power in witnessing, for "with great power gave the apostles witness of the resurrection of the Lord Jesus: and great grace was upon them all (Acts 4:33). The people were "pricked in their heart" until they cried out, "Men and brethren, what shall we do?" (Acts 2:37). With this, three thousand responded to the message to repent and were brought into the kingdom of God that day.

Stephen, "full of faith and power, did great wonders and miracles among the people" (Acts 6:8). As a result of his preaching, the people "were cut to the heart, and they gnashed on him with their teeth" (Acts 7:54), and finally stoned him to death. This probably was one of the greatest days in the history of the church, for out of this came the conversion of Saul (Paul) the apostle.

Philip, the deacon turned evangelist, knew that power when at his preaching the whole wicked city of Samaria turned to God and was filled with joy (Acts 8:5–8). Then he saw that glorious conversion of the Ethiopian eunuch. It has been a long time since a city like Samaria was moved by an evangelist.

Jesus knew such power. The Scriptures tell "how God anointed Jesus of Nazareth with the Holy Ghost and with power" (Acts 10:38). Rather than debate it, let us compare what we see today with what Jesus had. Whatever power is, most of us cry out to be anointed with it. As evangelist Vance Havner says, "Whatever it is, most of us don't have it." Power seems to be foreign to us today. Most of us want it. We all need it.

Paul said, "My speech and my preaching was not with enticing words of man's wisdom, but in demonstration of the Spirit and of power" (1 Cor. 2:4). Much preaching today is filled with beautiful rhetoric and oratory of persuasive speech but is powerless. Jonathan Edwards preached with such power that men gripped the pews, crying that they felt they were slipping into hell. Every man of God would long to see such conviction today.

To the Thessalonians Paul said, "For our gospel came not unto you in word only, but also in power, and in the Holy Ghost, and in much assurance" (1 Thess. 1:5). The gospel didn't come in word only, not just in conversation; it was not just so much talk. Paul did not just rattle on about Christ; something happened. The gospel came in power, conviction, and conversion. Corrupt Corinth needed to have the power of God. So it is today. No matter where your city is, it needs the power of God to see lives transformed. Thus his preaching came with confirmation in much "assurance." There will not always be the same results. Some will produce thirty, some sixty, and some one hundredfold (Matt. 13:23), but there must be the results that bear out the power of God.

Those who claim the power of Pentecost should have the people of Pentecost in conversions. That is, they should be seeing results of people witnessing and people converted. The power of Pentecost was to witness, not to worship. God says, "Ye shall receive power, . . . and ye shall be witnesses" (Acts 1:8). Any claim to what they had at Pentecost ought to bring the same results as Pentecost. Two primary results I see are disciples and doctrine. People were saved daily. They were not trying to get saints to have another Pentecost experience; they were witnessing for sinners to be saved.

Then they stressed doctrine: "they continued stedfastly in the apostles' doctrine" (Acts 2:42). There is far too much loose teaching today. You hear too much that people are not making issues over doctrine; they just believe in love. That is dangerous. There is a terrible hodgepodge of "fellowship" today. Doctrine is foundational.

No matter what the "experience" has been, how can a child of God "fellowship" with those who deny the blood of Christ or the deity of Christ or the accuracy and authority of the Word of God, and especially salvation by faith alone apart from works? God says, "Try the spirits." I'm afraid not enough of this is being done in many circles. There is much talk and preaching about the Holy Spirit today. Satan's method of counterfeiting the real thing is one of his devices. Born-again Christians need to be careful that they do not get caught up into an exciting and so-called "religious" experience that denies the fundamentals of the faith. Trace church history. None of the proven men of God of the past, such as D. L. Moody, Billy Sunday, C. H. Spurgeon, G. Campbell Morgan, Hudson Taylor, or Adoniram Judson, claimed such works of the Spirit with outward evidences as many claim today. We know their track record. Don't be carried away by some new wind of doctrine.

THE HOLY SPIRIT AND POWER

There is a real correlation between the Holy Spirit and power. Acts 1:8 pins it down clearly. In the Old Testament there is one account which speaks volumes for us today, and that is about Samson. Remember, what happened to Israel is an example for us to learn (see 1 Cor. 10:11). God tells us, "And the Spirit of the Lord began to move him at times"

(Judg. 13:25). God is beginning to move men today in unusual ways once again.

Power is associated with the Holy Spirit coming upon Samson: "And the Spirit of the Lord came mightily upon him, and he rent him [the lion] as he would rent a kid, and he had nothing in his hand" (Judg. 14:6). It would seem that the Holy Spirit coming upon Samson is different from the Holy Spirit indwelling believers today. It seems from this passage and many others like it that the Holy Spirit comes upon them in possession and power. God just completely takes over that person. He is truly beside himself. As God said of Saul, "Thou . . . shalt be turned into another man" (1 Sam. 10:6).

The Holy Spirit came upon Samson again, and he went down to Ashkelon and slew thirty men (see Judg. 14:19). When Samson was bound with cords, "the Spirit of the Lord came mightily upon him, and the cords that were upon his arms became as flax that was burnt with fire" (Judg. 15:14). What physical power he had! This power was far more than he had had as a human being. It was a supernatural strength.

Notice in Judges 16:20 when "the Lord was departed from him," Samson was as weak as any other man. The total difference was the Holy Spirit upon him in power. Spirit-called and Spirit-filled preachers can tell you about preaching with the Holy Spirit coming in power and the difference it makes. Some preachers never know this thrilling and sacred experience of preaching in the power of the Holy Spirit, but it is real. How does it happen? When does it happen? What must be done to see it happen?

PRAYER AND POWER

"Tarry ye in the city of Jerusalem," said Jesus, "until ye be endued with power from on high" (Luke 24:49). Pentecost would have been fulfilled according to the feasts of Jehovah of Leviticus 23, no matter what anyone did. The Holy Spirit would have come. Believers would have received the Holy Spirit.

But this enduement with power that they saw in evidence through their preaching would not have been theirs had they not spent those days in one accord in one place in prayer. There is a definite correlation between prayer and power. If we had more praying in private, we would have more power in public. Prayer brings power. Little prayer, little power; much prayer, much power. Any preacher who knows anything about prayer and preaching knows this is so. We see so little power because we do so little praying.

There is a correlation between boldness and power. Early Christians prayed for boldness and got power: "And now, Lord, behold their threatenings: and grant unto thy servants, that with all boldness they may speak thy word, . . . and when they had prayed, the place was shaken where they were assembled together; and they were all filled with the Holy Ghost, and they spake the word of God with boldness" (Acts 4:29-31). You already have the Holy Spirit if you are born again, but when you pray for Him to get hold of you, you see the power of God.

The most sacred and unusual period of my life happened while I was pastoring in Pensacola, Florida. I became burdened to see the power of God demonstrated in my preaching and my ministry. My ultimate goal was the winning of the lost to Christ and seeing them transformed. I prayed for boldness and power. God brought to my mind to be "abandoned to Christ." I did this, not concerned about what anyone said or did. All I wanted was to see God do something that could not be explained by human standards. We saw it. Scores were being saved and transformed. People didn't just join the church. Their whole lives were being changed in a moment. It became the talk of the town.

A pastor stopped me on the street one day and asked, "Wemp, what are you doing in that church that so much is happening?" I was so aware that God was doing it, I burst into tears and could hardly speak. Of course, I told him God did it; I had nothing to do with it at all. Another pastor said he was going to get a pulpit supply to preach for him one Sunday and slip into our church because he had heard of so much happening. God gave me a new boldness, not brashness, I had never had before. I have found in my preaching and witnessing ever since that there is a definite connection between boldness and power.

PERSECUTION AND POWER

Three times Paul prayed for the thorn in his flesh to be removed. God did not remove it, but told him His grace was sufficient. Then Paul said, "Most gladly therefore will I rather glory in my infirmities, that the power of Christ may rest upon me" (2 Cor. 12:9). Whatever the thorn, Paul knew there was a relationship between this thorn and the power of Christ upon him.

All through the Book of Acts there is a relationship between persecution and power. Many saints of the past carried a deep hurt and wounds throughout their lives that the power of Christ might be upon them. Don't run from pain and persecution. It may be the vehicle through which the power of Christ will be upon you.

Pray for power. Whatever else a person has, especially a preacher, he needs the power of God to accomplish anything for God. Don't be satisfied with anything less than a supernatural ministry. Don't settle for less than what God wants you to have. "There is none that . . . stirreth up himself to take hold of [God]" (Isa. 64:7). Don't let this be said of you. Cry out night and day until you have that sweet anointing of God in power.

John W. Peterson has expressed it perfectly in what I think is his greatest song:

The Holy Spirit came at Pentecost;
He came in mighty fullness then.
His witness through believers won the lost
And multitudes were born again.

How on Earth Can I Have the Power of God?

The early Christians scattered o'er the world;
They preached the gospel fearlessly.
Though some were martyred and to lions hurled,
They marched along in victory.

Then in an age when darkness gripped the earth,
The just shall live by faith was learned.
The Holy Spirit gave the church new birth
As Reformation fires burned.

In later years revival fires came,
When saints would seek the Lord and pray.
But once again we need that holy flame
To meet the challenge of today.

Come, Holy Spirit, dark is the hour.
We need your filling, your love and your mighty power.
Move now among us, stir us we pray.
Come, Holy Spirit, revive the church today.*

Study Questions: Chapter 17

1. Discuss the power of God in Christians and churches today.
2. What are some statements in Scripture about the power of the Holy Spirit in the early church?
3. What was the power of Pentecost intended to be for? How was it fulfilled?
4. What can be learned about the power of the Holy Spirit through living?
5. What are the relationships between power, prayer, and boldness?

*COME HOLY SPIRIT, by John W. Peterson © Copyright 1971 by Singspiration, Inc. All rights reserved. Used by permission.

18
When on Earth
Is Jesus Coming?

"I will come again, and receive you unto myself; that where I am, there ye may be also" (John 14:3). Make no mistake, He is coming again. What a blessed thought! He is preparing a place especially for us. Heaven is a place and not a figment of imagination. Life doesn't end here; it only begins. What a place heaven will be!

Jesus ascended in the sight of His apostles, "and while they looked stedfastly toward heaven as he went up, behold, two men stood by them in white apparel; which also said, Ye men of Galilee, why stand ye gazing up into heaven? this same Jesus, which is taken up from you into heaven, shall so come in like manner as ye have seen him go into heaven" (Acts 1:10,11). "This same Jesus" is coming. Isn't that exciting? I've been to the Holy Land five times. I was thrilled to walk where Jesus walked and imagined being with Him by the Sea of Galilee. Better than just imagining it, one day I am going to see this same Jesus, and then we will never part. What a day that will be!

"Behold, I shew you a mystery; We shall not all sleep, but we shall all be changed, in a moment, in the twinkling of an eye, at the last trump: for the trumpet shall sound, and the dead shall be raised incorruptible and we shall all be changed" (1 Cor. 15:51,52). "We shall not all sleep." This is a most startling revelation, and it staggers one's imagination. Many will be alive when Jesus comes and will be changed in a moment without ever dying. This truth can keep our hearts pounding with joy and anticipation.

How is it going to happen? "For the Lord himself shall descend from heaven with a shout, with the voice of the archangel, and with the trump of God: and the dead in Christ shall rise first: Then we which are alive and remain shall be caught up together with them in the clouds, to meet the Lord in the air: and so shall we ever be with the Lord. Wherefore comfort one another with these words" (1 Thess 4:16-18). What a comforting hope. Our loved ones who have died before us shall rise first, and then together we who are in Christ shall be caught up to meet the Lord in the air. What a reunion! That will be one meeting you won't want to miss. There will be singing and shouting as you have never heard before.

Our daughter Carolyn had spent the summer in Spain visiting mission fields. It seemed like an awfully long summer. My wife, our daughter Janet, and I drove to New York to meet Carolyn. We hardly slept the night before her arrival because we were so excited. All day we counted the hours and finally the minutes till her arrival. At Kennedy Airport we watched the Swiss airplanes land for more than an hour anxiously waiting. Finally, having been told her plane was landing, we went to the customs door to await her arrival. We saw people, one after another, coming through the door and meeting loved ones. People were hugging and weeping all around us. The anticipation was almost unbearable. Several people came through and had no one to meet them; one young lady looked disappointed. It seemed so sad. The door swung open, and at last there came our Carolyn. Janet, then 12 years old, rushed into her arms, the tears streaming down her face. They kissed and hugged and wept. I just stood watching and weeping. It seemed she would never get to me. Finally we met face to face and grabbed each other. Beaming and weeping, I said, "Welcome home, Carolyn." Like a bolt of lightning it hit me. Not only had she been anxiously looking forward to seeing us, but I could hardly wait to see my child! I had never before realized how God must be feeling now as He waits to see us face to face. I burst into tears and shared with my family: "Just think, the dear Lord can hardly wait to see us too!" That fantastic thought has flooded my soul with joy now for several years. The coming of the Lord Jesus is just the greatest thing that can happen to us.

WHAT WILL HAPPEN WHEN JESUS COMES?

First and foremost, we are going to see Jesus and be like Him. My life's verse says, "Beloved, now are we the sons of God, and it doth not yet appear what we shall be: but we know that, when he shall appear, we shall be like him; for we shall see him as he is" (1 John 3:2). We are going to see Him as He is. Well, *glory!* This is it. This is the ultimate. When I hear people become all excited about walking on streets of gold, I get an empty feeling. Gold just won't mean a thing. What will matter then will be only Jesus. We are going to see Him in all His beauty and glory. We are going to see the One who loved us and died for us. Believe me, we won't run up to Him and slap Him on the back shouting, "Glad to see you!" Oh, no! We will fall at His feet in glorious adoration for a million years or so. There just aren't words enough to describe what that moment will be like, but it will be the greatest moment of all time for every believer.

Then, glory to God, we shall be like Him. This is the heart cry of every discerning child of God today. Aren't you tired of sin and failure? Doesn't it crush you to see the weakness of the flesh and the shallowness of our love for God? One day, dear friend, we will be perfect and have the capacity to love Him perfectly and gloriously. No more sin. No more emptiness. No more failure. No more barriers. Just perfect love and fellowship. No wonder God says, "And everyone that hath this hope in him purifieth himself, even as he is pure" (1 John 3:3). If anything will cause a Christian to live a holy life, this will. Do you have this hope, this expectation, this anticipation, burning in your heart?

Then, we shall be rewarded. "Behold, I come quickly; and my reward is with me, to give every man according as his work shall be" (Rev. 22:12). Yes, there are rewards to be gained. It makes a lot of difference how you live after you are saved. It is just plain stupid to say, "Once saved, always saved," and live any way you please. No, you can't. God will spank you if you do, as we are told in Hebrews 12 and 1

Corinthians 11:29ff. You will also suffer loss of rewards. First Corinthians 3:11ff. tells us our works are to be tried by fire. If they are built out of wood, hay, or stubble, they will be burned up, and you will get no reward. If they are built out of gold, silver, or precious stones, you will get a reward.

Wood could represent works done for our own praise. God says, "Whatsoever ye do, do all to the glory of God" (1 Cor. 10:31). Those who do their works to be "seen of men, Verily I say unto you, They have their reward" (Matt. 6:5). That's an awfully cheap payoff. Why not do your works for the glory of God and receive an eternal reward? Why settle for less?

Hay could be works done other than in the name of Jesus. "And whatsoever ye do in word or deed, do all in the name of the Lord Jesus, giving thanks to God and the Father by him" (Col. 3:17). I'm a Baptist, but I must not do my works as a Baptist or in the name of the Baptists, but only as a Christian in the name of the Lord Jesus. I cringe when I hear people answer the question, "Are you a Christian?" by saying, "I'm a Baptist" or "a Methodist" or "a Catholic." Only those in Christ will be in heaven, and only what's done in His name will bring reward.

The stubble could be the works not done in love. "Though I speak with the tongues of men and angels, and have not [love], I am become as sounding brass, or a tinkling cymbal. . . . And though I bestow all my goods to feed the poor, and though I give my body to be burned, and have not [love], it profiteth me nothing" (1 Cor. 13:1–3). A lot of good deeds are going up in smoke because they aren't done in love. If the reality of this were to break through to all believers, it could revolutionize our Christian service. What a joy witnessing and Christian service is when done in genuine love. It brings eternal dividends.

Gold characterized the holy places of the tabernacle, the places of worship. When the three kings came to worship the newborn Babe, they brought gold. Spending time on our knees in absolute adoration of the Lord of glory brings a blessing here and a great reward hereafter. 'The Father seeketh such to worship him" (John 4:23). There just isn't enough worship of the Lord Jesus in public or private.

The silver can represent the price of redemption or witnessing. "And all things are of God, who . . . hath given to us the ministry of reconciliation; to wit, that God was in Christ, reconciling the world unto himself, not imputing their trespasses unto them; and hath committed unto us the word of reconciliation. Now then we are ambassadors for Christ, as though God did beseech you by us: we pray you in Christ's stead, be ye reconciled to God" (2 Cor. 5:18–20). Christ has done the work of reconciliation. We now have the word of reconciliation committed to us. "How shall they hear without a preacher?" (Rom. 10:14). "He that winneth souls is wise" (Prov. 11:30), for soul-winning brings blessing now and eternal rewards hereafter.

Precious stones made the breastplate of the priests as they went before the Lord. On each stone was carved the name of one of the tribes of Israel. God says, "And Aaron shall bear the names of the children of Israel in the breastplate of judgment upon his heart, when he goeth in unto the holy place, for a memorial before the Lord continually" (Exod. 28:29). This seems to indicate intercession. It is wonderful to bear the names of people on our hearts before the Lord.

Jake and Dolly Lyons have born my name on their hearts and prayed for me almost daily for thirty-five years. They have had a greater part and effect on my ministry than anyone else in the world. Intercession is a great service. Don't neglect it.

"The fire shall try every man's work of what sort it is. If any man's work abide which he hath built thereupon, he shall receive a reward. If any man's work shall be burned, he shall suffer loss: but he himself shall be saved; yet so as by fire" (1 Cor. 3:13–15). What a tragedy to go to heaven, emptyhanded, "yet so as by fire." Saved, yes, but nothing to show for all of his life.

There will be rewards in the form of crowns. In the Greek games the winners were given the laurels or crowns of wreaths placed on their heads by the emperors. So one day the King of Kings will pass out crowns to those who have run the race and finished the course.

"Blessed is the man that endureth temptation: for when he is tried, he shall receive the crown of life, which the Lord hath promised to them that love him" (James 1:12). Think of it as a crown of life for those who endure temptation or testing. The idea of enduring means to pass the test with flying colors, not just to put up with the testing. No wonder God says, "Count it all joy when ye fall into divers temptations" (James 1:2). Are you going through deep waters? Is the cross heavy to bear? "Count it all joy." Don't fret; don't faint. "In everything give thanks" (1 Thess. 5:18), "For great is your reward in heaven" (Matt. 5:12).

There is a "crown of glory" for those who feed the flock of God with the right attitude and for the right purpose (1 Pet. 5:4). This has special reference to pastors, many of whom are paid little here. Many give out much and endure a lot here, but there is "a crown of glory that fadeth not away."

Men train and work and run races here for a corruptible crown. One of my neighbors ran five to ten miles every day to train for a race. I admired him, but his reward here was nothing compared to the incorruptible crown for those who keep their body under subjection (1 Cor. 9:24–27) and run the race God has for them. Too many never even enter the race. Another larger number break the rules and are disqualified from the race. Thank God, many finish the race and win the prize!

There is a "crown of rejoicing." "For what is our hope, or joy, or crown of rejoicing? Are not even ye in the presence of our Lord Jesus Christ at his coming?" (1 Thess. 2:19). Years ago I led a high school boy to Christ. God called him to be an evangelist. He has been greatly used. He is my "crown of rejoicing now"; but there is an eternal crown for the souls we have won to Christ.

Finally there is a crown of righteousness for those who have finished their course and who love His appearing. "I have fought a good fight, I have finished my course, I have kept the faith: Henceforth there is laid up for me a crown of righteousness, which the Lord, the righteous judge, shall give me at that day: and not to me only, but unto all them also that love his appearing" (2 Tim. 4:7,8).

God doesn't leave us here to see just how good we can be or just to sit. He has a plan and purpose for each life. There is a race to be run and a fight to be fought. Most of us get weary, but you just can't quit. Satan doesn't. No one can afford the luxury of self-indulgence or self-pity, for souls are dying daily. God says, "Be not weary in well doing: for in due season we shall reap, if we faint not" (Gal. 6:9). There will be a harvest here and a reward hereafter. No one who is backslidden will love His appearing. Anyone with unconfessed sin will try to hide, as did Adam, and "be ashamed before him at his coming" (1 John 2:28). Here is one crown they won't have. "Look to yourselves, that we lose not those things which we have wrought, but that we receive a full reward" (2 John 8).

What will we do with all these crowns? Will some pile them up one on top of the other and parade around heaven with them? Will there be any glorying in our rewards? Of course not. There will be one grand and glorious act with the crowns. "The four and twenty elders fall down before him that sat on the throne, and worship him that liveth for ever and ever, and cast their crowns before the throne, saying, Thou art worthy, O Lord, to receive glory and honor and power: for thou hast created all things, and for thy pleasure they are and were created" (Rev. 4:10,11). What a fantastic moment. What a thrilling thought that we shall lay our trophies at Jesus' feet and bring honor and glory to Him.

My father has over fifty trophies that he has won in bowling. It is a tribute to his working at it and his faithfulness to bowling over the years. You walk into his house and you are impressed with the sight of these trophies. What an impressive sight when our blessed Lord shall have the myriad of trophies at His feet. How sad the thought of a born-again, blood-washed saint not having one trophy to lay at Jesus' feet.

How in the world can I be spiritual? By realizing I am the sacred temple of the Holy Spirit and letting Him do all He came to do. How? By realizing I'm going to give an account of every deed done in the body, whether good or bad (2 Cor. 5:10). How? By realizing I'm going to see Jesus face to face and be like Him one day. For "every man that hath this hope in him purifieth himself, even as he is pure" (1 John 3:3).

Study Questions: Chapter 18

1. Discuss the truth of Christians wanting to see the Lord, and He wanting to see them!
2. What is going to happen when Jesus comes?
3. What do wood, hay, and stubble represent?
4. What do gold, silver, and precious stones represent?
5. What are the crowns to be won? How are they won?
6. What will believers do with crowns in heaven?